Nov 2007

Peace on the Path

Discover
Your
Spiritual
Life

Your
Paul,
Coach
&
Confidant

About the Author

Elizabeth Owens is a certified medium and an ordained Spiritualist minister. She teaches spiritual development classes in the Cassadaga Spiritualist Camp in Cassadaga, Florida, where she also resides.

To Write to the Author

If you wish to contact the author or would like more information about this book, please write to the author in care of Llewellyn Worldwide and we will forward your request. Both the author and publisher appreciate hearing from you and learning of your enjoyment of this book and how it has helped you. Llewellyn Worldwide cannot guarantee that every letter written to the author can be answered, but all will be forwarded. Please write to:

Elizabeth Owens
℅ Llewellyn Worldwide
P.O. Box 64383, Dept. 0-7387-0423-7
St. Paul, MN 55164-0383, U.S.A.

Please enclose a self-addressed stamped envelope for reply, or $1.00 to cover costs. If outside U.S.A., enclose international postal reply coupon.

Many of Llewellyn's authors have websites with additional information and resources. For more information, please visit our website at http://www.llewellyn.com.

Discover Your Spiritual Life

Illuminate Your Soul's Path

Elizabeth Owens

2004
Llewellyn Publications
St. Paul, Minnesota 55164-0383, U.S.A.

First Edition
First Printing, 2004

Book design and editing by Karin Simoneau
Cover art © 2004 Neil Beer / Getty Images
Cover design by Lisa Novak

Library of Congress Cataloging-in-Publication Data
Owens, Elizabeth, 1948–
  Discover your spiritual life: illuminate your soul's path /
  Elizabeth Owens
    p. cm.
  Includes bibliographical references.
  ISBN 0-7387-0423-7
  I. Spiritual life. I. Title.

  BL624.092 2003
  294'.4—dc22   2003065694

Llewellyn Worldwide does not participate in, endorse, or have any authority or responsibility concerning private business transactions between our authors and the public.

All mail addressed to the author is forwarded but the publisher cannot, unless specifically instructed by the author, give out an address or phone number.

Any Internet references contained in this work are current at publication time, but the publisher cannot guarantee that a specific location will continue to be maintained. Please refer to the publisher's website for links to authors' websites and other sources.

Llewellyn Publications
A Division of Llewellyn Worldwide, Ltd.
P.O. Box 64383, Dept. 0-7387-0423-7
St. Paul, MN 55164-0383, U.S.A.
www.llewellyn.com

Printed in the United States of America

Other Books by Elizabeth Owens

Women Celebrating Life: A Guide to Growth and Transformation

How to Communicate with Spirits

To George P. Colby, founder of the Southern Cassadaga Spiritualist Camp, Cassadaga, Florida.

Contents

Acknowledgments

My friend, Miriam Withers, of the National League of American Pen Women, DeLand, Florida Branch, thank you so very much for editing my manuscript. Your keen eye and knowledge were a blessing. Many thanks to you for sharing your talents!

My thanks also to Kristy Westbrook and June Schmitt, who allowed me to share some of their life experiences. What great women!

To my buddy, Carol Roberts—I am so blessed to know you. Thank you so much for sharing your experiences with me—and the world. But especially, thanks for being such a wonderful friend.

Thank you, Arlene Sikora, for the reading that preceded the creation of this book. You'll never know how much it helped me.

My appreciation to Diane Davis for her friendship. You are always there for me.

Big hugs to you, Marie Lilla, you sweetheart! You are one of the kindest ladies I know.

Many thanks to Nancy Mostad, Lisa Braun, and Karin Simoneau at Llewellyn Worldwide. These ladies made it all happen!

A *huge* thank-you to all the lovely people who e-mailed me with compliments and questions about *How to Communicate with Spirits*. I love corresponding with you and greatly appreciate your enjoyment of all my books. After all, I write these books for you!

Last, but not least, my husband always receives recognition when I complete a book because his support is so necessary in seeing any project to completion. Thank you, Sweetie! I love you!

Introduction

When we feel inspired to pursue a more spiritual path in our lives, we usually have a desire to reach out and connect with something we regard as spiritual, be it called God, Goddess, Spirit, Mother Earth, or something else. We seek higher guidance to find the answers to troubling questions that appear to have no concrete answers. Some of us do not find the comfort we require inside a church building, nor does religion in general seem to hold the answers we seek. Where does one turn for help? Inside. Within each of us is that spark of God, Goddess, or whatever title you choose, waiting to assist us in our spiritual journey. We can reach in and make the connection if we truly want to do so. What we will receive as a result cannot be measured in material items we can hold in our hands. Mainly, it will be felt within our hearts.

This book is designed for the beginning seeker. You will find it to be composed in a straightforward, easy-to-read manner, with simple instructions and suggestions for a more spiritual way to live. By cultivating a different understanding and acquiring a new perception of circumstances, we can learn how to handle problems and disappointments. In so doing, we become Balanced Observers instead of concerned worriers.

Imagine a large rock in the middle of a river. Water is streaming toward the rock, much the way life bombards us at times with problems and irritations. When the water hits the rock, it is deflected to either side. The rock knows that the water striking it cannot damage its interior. The water simply rolls around the body of the rock and flows away. Eventually, the same water disperses and blends into the rest of the water in the river, a vague memory to the rock. Realizing that this transition will happen in all future circumstances, the rock does not take issue with the water when it streams at it again. The rock remains balanced, observing the flow. This is the Balanced Observer.

One of the most important lessons we learn during our incarnation is how to accept and react to the life lessons we are asked to grow through. Right thinking and right action are two tools that assist in our growth. We must strive to develop an open and flexible attitude when we meet with obstacles on our spiritual paths during our spiritual walk. We are able to accomplish much on our spiritual journey through daily meditation, prayer, and learning the power of our thoughts and the correct usage of words so we may have a positive affect on the Universe. As a result, we will realize how limited our individual perceptions have been.

Let us look at the relationship between identical twins named Kim and Konnie as an example of how skewed our perceptions can be. Each twin thought the other sister had the better life. Kim jealously saw Konnie as the fortunate one because she was married to a nice man, and had a lovely house, a nice car, and two beautiful children. These were all things Kim wanted desperately in her own life.

Konnie, on the other hand, saw her twin as the one who was blessed. Konnie viewed Kim as being independent, self-sufficient, and free to do whatever she pleased. Kim's status of singlehood and her accomplishments in her career appeared very appealing compared to the day-to-day responsibilities of running a household and taking care of children.

After years of resentment toward each other, the twins finally sat down to discuss what was causing their differences. When they compared notes, both were surprised that the other was jealous of her situation. While Konnie thought Kim had everything a woman could want, she never realized the strong desire Kim had for children. Kim had suffered silently through a bad marriage and divorce, and then projected her energy into her career. Her struggle up the corporate ladder had been difficult and lonely. Konnie was totally surprised by this realization.

Konnie didn't appreciate her life because she blamed marital responsibilities and motherhood for preventing her from attending college and starting a career. Therefore, a life as a single person gave the appearance of being easier and freer. It was easier for Konnie to be jealous of her sister than it was for her to take responsibility for her decision to create a family instead of the major effort it would have taken to have both a career and a family. Kim was living the life that Konnie wanted to experience and Konnie was living the life that Kim desired! Each twin coveted what the other sister had, perceiving the opposite life as her ideal. The twins did not realize the difficulties associated with the other's life because their view was skewed by individual perception. Neither life was actually wrong or right, better or worse. It was all perception.

When we follow our newly realized and changing perceptions, forgiveness is paramount to our spiritual growth. We receive a healing when we learn to forgive those who have harmed us. In most of the chapters you will find a "to-do list" and exercises that are designed to help cultivate this new understanding, changed perception, and forgiveness. All these practices will help you to become a Balanced Observer.

Our purpose for being on earth is to provide our souls with ample opportunities for growth. We are given many situations in which to experience happiness, sadness, joy, hope, disappointment, grief, anger, jealousy, revenge, and confusion, to name just a few human emotions. If we can learn to recognize these situations that are presented to us as our opportunities for spiritual growth and, dare I suggest, appreciate their existence, we will live happier lives. In this small recognition of a growth opportunity, we are turning unpleasant situations into positive ones.

As we grow through our spiritual journey on earth, we are challenged to treat nature and all living creatures with love, respect, and kindness. My observation of our society as a whole is that our behavior isn't working. We don't show a lot of respect and we certainly aren't kind to each other. As long as we still have wars, we aren't being loving, kind, or respectful of each other.

Remember when you were a child and your mother would tell you, "Play nice"? Why can't we play nice with each other? Why does each of us always have to be right? A popular phrase is "Would you rather be right or happy?" Personally, I would choose to be happy any day of the week. By the time we reach adulthood, we should have learned how to get along with each other. Building a spiritual path may help some people to achieve a more open, tolerant demeanor.

Society hasn't raised its level of tolerance high enough yet, either. People march in protest for the rights of others to attract our attention, and to educate us, but most of us still do not openly embrace each other's differences. There isn't anything loving, kind, or respectful about intolerance. We have to do better. If we could just learn to see beyond what our individual limited vision affords us, our potential for growth would be unlimited.

Our perception of events, situations, and beliefs is very important to our spiritual growth. By recognizing that there are different ways to view any one thing, we can change our lives for the better. We also gain a greater understanding of others. When we limit ourselves to one viewpoint, we are cheating ourselves of growth and of having a new experience.

What I offer within these pages is for your consideration. My way is not necessarily your way; that's what makes us individuals. Some of the suggestions in this book may appear as new thoughts, while others may have a familiarity, depending upon your previous exposure. I would ask that you read my words with an open heart and an open mind. Allow yourself to be exposed to something new. If some of the concepts seem foreign or naive, mull them over for a period of time. If you open your heart, you will find a lot of truth in these words.

In my directions for seeking a more spiritual way to live, I offer ideal situations as I see them. Not everyone can acquire the ideal due to family or personal tastes. However, my ideal is not important. What is important is that you do what is acceptable and comfortable for you personally. That is your ideal. We are all blessed with free will and should exercise our free will when something appears that does not harmonize with our being. For instance, when referring to a higher being, if I use a title that you are not comfortable with, then I encourage you to change the title to one that is meaningful to you. If a suggestion feels contrary to your family situation, adjust the suggestion to favor your circumstances.

The goal is to find a spiritual path that is suited to your highest and best spiritual growth. This book is a good starting point. You may wish to use it as groundwork for expansion to other avenues of spiritual pursuit. I would further suggest that you borrow pieces to construct your personal spiritual path from wherever you find something that resonates within your being. Take a block from Christianity, a stone from Buddhism, and a brick from Taoism, and cement them together with love to form your personal spiritual path. Every book you read will add a pebble to your path. The choice is yours to make.

I sincerely wish you a happy, healthy journey into the world of spirituality. May it be a blessed path that enlightens you, guides you, and fulfills your spiritual needs.

Chapter 1

Seeking a Better Way

At some point in our lives, many of us are drawn to cultivate a more spiritual way to live. Perhaps there's an emptiness inside that is crying out to be filled with some indefinable something that will be the catalyst to our seeking a new and better way to subsist. Maybe it is because of a death in the family, a divorce, the realization of our own mortality, or because everyone else we know seems to be happier than we are. Sometimes the interest in beginning our spiritual path is brought on by a mystical experience. We are given a glimpse, a moment of clarity, that there is more to life than what we have discovered so far in our material existence. Whatever the reason, suddenly, we want more meaning in our lives.

If this is where you presently find yourself, welcome; you're not alone and, even better, it's normal to feel this way. Congratulations, you're *normal!* Just as an adopted child will usually have a curiosity and yearning to find his or her birth parents, so is it natural for us to carry a desire to reconnect to our Source, the source of our creation. Whether we call that creative energy God, Goddess, Higher Power, Infinite Intelligence, Spirit, the Universe, or something else—it is our source of life. It is that tiny spiritual spark that resides inside all of us, that special inner connectedness to a Supreme Being. We want to know more about It, we want to be closer to this Being, and we want to feel the influence of the Supreme Life Force within us. We desire a more spiritual existence that will bring us peace and fulfillment. We deserve to have this in our lives. What's more, it is the desire of the Universe that we receive it.

For Abby, her spiritual quest began during a period of time when her dreams became precognitive; basic messages contained in her dreams would play out in real life. She dreamed about a coworker being ill. Within two days, the person she had dreamed about announced at work that he had just discovered he had a serious illness. Abby's grandmother came to her in a dream to say goodbye. Abby's mother called her the next morning to tell Abby that her grandmother had died. A friend of Abby's had an auto accident a few days after Abby had foreseen it in her dreams. Understandably, these events caused Abby much concern. She became afraid to go to sleep at night.

In hopes of finding an explanation, Abby sought the services of a medium. The medium told Abby that she was very psychic and a naturally sensitive woman. Since she did not practice meditation, Abby's spirit teachers were communicating with her through her dreams, the only means left open to them.

Abby asked why they were sending her such negative dreams? She was told that it was to get her attention. She would give more attention to dreams in which unpleasant occurrences were predicted than she would give to happy dreams. Abby said she didn't care what the motives of the spirits were, she didn't want those dreams to continue!

The medium advised Abby that if she were to meditate, she would find that her dreams would change. The spirits only desired to communicate with Abby, to guide her life in a positive fashion, not scare her. The medium went on to say that Abby was very gifted and that this was all part of a master plan in which she was meant to help people. This type of mystical experience is not uncommon, and was the catalyst to Abby's spiritual search.

Sometimes people are confused about religion and spirituality. Please understand, they are not the same. People may attend church regularly, go through all the motions of practicing their chosen faith, yet not be demonstrating spiritual aspects during their daily affairs. Other times, people are so caught up in religious dogma that it blocks rational thinking. They adopt a rigid perspective, a black-and-white approach to life, unaware that by accepting the rigidity of a belief they are turning their back on the unconditional love that God, Goddess, and the Universe intended us to share with everyone.

Spirituality is more than a belief one holds. It is carrying that belief into action, demonstrating to others a behavior. Spirituality is a behavior, not a religion. Many highly spiritual beings do not choose to attend church because they believe spirituality is not found exclusively in church. A church is merely a building. Just because we enter a structure called a church or practice a certain religion doesn't make us spiritual. Don't we all know some folks who consistently go to church on Sunday, raise hell all week, and then return to church the next Sunday just so they can receive forgiveness for the previous week's sins? The proof of spirituality is demonstrated by how we treat humans, animals, and the environment.

To profess love for our fellow humans when we are inside a church and then step outside and curse the existence of a particular race is not demonstrating spirituality. To say we are open and tolerant of all people and then turn around and judge someone with a different sexual persuasion is not demonstrating spirituality. Spirituality is putting into practice our beliefs, a loving demonstration of our beliefs.

As an example, let's take two friends who are both devout Christians. One is constantly trying to improve herself and truly demonstrates truth by her actions. She walks and talks her beliefs daily. Most people would consider her a very spiritual person. The other woman is married to a minister and talks a good story, preaching to anyone within earshot about proper decorum. Behind the scenes, the criticism and negativity that this person spews is anything but spiritual. The worst part is that the minister's wife doesn't realize that she would be wise to listen to her own preaching, or that of her husband's!

Divorce was the catalyst that propelled Vincent into seeking spirituality. Vincent's personal situation posed questions to which he needed answers. He also required emotional healing. Two friends, Patsy and John, brought Vincent to a weeknight service in the church at the Cassadaga Spiritualist Camp, in Florida, where he was exposed to spiritual messages being delivered publicly by mediums. The threesome also began attending Sunday church services, where they were introduced to a different philosophy and perspective about life.

John was highly skeptical at first, thinking that this was just hocus-pocus. He had led somewhat of a promiscuous life to that point, and also tended to think negatively. On the other hand, Patsy was a full believer in what she witnessed from the very beginning. Vincent was fascinated with what he saw and, much to his delight, received messages every time he attended services. He really valued those messages and found that they helped him cross from a place of pain into a new life with hope.

The three friends continued to attend services regularly, which inspired them to join the psychic development and Natural Law classes that were being held in the town. While Vincent participated with his friends in psychic development classes, he did not choose to pursue a vocation in mediumship. However, he has found those lessons in spiritual behavior to be invaluable to him in the years since his exposure.

Patsy and John both eventually became mediums, with John changing his life patterns dramatically. He became very cautious about what he said about people, never wanting to say anything negative or derogatory, and his thinking went from a negative thought pattern to a very positive one.

I never cared much about attending church as an adult, nor did I have any interest in religion. I only attended church services at Christmas and Easter. My indifference was likely due to the fact that my mother made me go to church on Sundays when I was young, when all I wanted to do after a week of school was sleep. It wasn't until I received a psychic reading that I became interested in a spiritual path, which eventually led me to the same Spiritualist church that the aforementioned trio attended. It was there that I found a religion that would give me the satisfaction and comfort I needed, Spiritualism. It changed my perspective about everything: people, the earth, so-called bad occurrences, relationships, behaviors, illness—you name it, my thoughts changed.

To build a spiritual path, you do not have to be a Spiritualist. Let me state that clearly so no one thinks I'm on a bandwagon proselytizing. As I said before, spirituality is *not* about religion. It is putting a belief into practice, demonstrating truth. One can be of any faith or no faith at all and still be a spiritual person. You may be surprised to know that the clerk behind the deli counter at your grocery store might be living a spiritual life that would put some ministers to shame. We have all read in the newspapers and tabloids about "ministers gone wrong" or the molestation of children by some Catholic priests. These are individuals who acted in poor judgment as they followed their baser instincts, all the while preaching a tune entirely different from the one they were dancing to. And they got caught. Appearances can frequently be deceiving when, not knowing the entire story, we only observe people's images.

Some people think you have to wear purple to be spiritual. That makes as much sense as the lady who uses scented bath products because she believes they will bring her feelings of tranquility and peace of mind. Spirituality isn't about what we wear, how we smell, or even that we meditate daily. What are we doing the rest of the day? How are we treating people the rest of the day? Try not to categorize who is and who isn't spiritual by the outside packaging. We all have the capacity to walk spiritual paths, and sometimes the last person we would imagine living a spiritual life is doing so to his or her fullest capacity, unbeknownst to us.

When Sonia's mother passed away, she mourned her loss severely. Sonia had always been very close to her mother, and missed their nightly telephone conversations. At seven o'clock every night, Sonia would cry because that was when she used to talk to her mother on the phone. To add to her grief, Sonia suddenly realized that she wasn't getting any younger herself. How many more years did she have? Sonia mourned her mother and her own loss of youth.

Eventually, Sonia began to read some spiritual books to assist in healing her emotions. What she read soothed her feelings, gave her comfort, and inspired her to continue reading spiritual books. Sonia began investigating different religions and frequenting used bookstores for more reading material. As a result of her mother's death, Sonia began seeking a spiritual path.

Is it easy to build a spiritual path and live it? That depends upon the individual. No, it isn't easy for some. Do spiritual people mess up? Yes, of course they do. Do spiritual people ever act in anger? You bet they do!

In the Bible there is a story about Jesus getting angry with the moneychangers in the temple. If Jesus was able to be overcome with anger, what chance do we have of never succumbing to anger? The point here is that we are human beings. We act passionately when something happens that we feel is wrong or unjust. We can't help it. But when something occurs that is distasteful and inappropriate, like monetary exchange in a temple, one sometimes has to take a stand and be heard. Jesus was not a wimp. He was passionate. Sometimes anger is used to get attention, to make a point, and from that outburst comes necessary change. However, it is never correct to hurt someone verbally or physically when we are outraged. Violent behavior is a demonstration of passion out of control. Jesus was not out of control.

The "ministers gone wrong" had their strengths tested and found it difficult to demonstrate spirituality when met with temptation, as did the priests. It is important to remember that human beings are imperfect, except for their souls. We have come to the earth to experience life and, in doing so, we learn. While free will is our blessing, there is a flipside to that coin. Free will also provides us with the freedom to make choices that aren't always in our best interests or those of other's. We cannot expect to make perfect choices every time. We cannot expect to behave in an ideal manner consistently. If we believe we must be perfect, we are only setting ourselves up for failure and disappointment. But we can *try*. We can aspire to behave in a manner that will make us proud of ourselves. If we sometimes miss the rung on the ladder of life, well, at least we tried. We still have the option to reach out again and get it right the next time. Consequently, we learn from our mistakes and are better for it.

Mistakes are interesting life experiences. We don't want to make mistakes, yet we do and we must. It's like a mother and her child. The mother protects her child, guiding and instructing the youngster until he or she is old enough to begin making his or her own decisions. But sometimes we do a disservice to our offspring by overprotecting them, thus preventing their learning from experiences.

"Listen to me. I know, I've been there. A true friend wouldn't ask you to do that," the mother might say.

Ah, but the teenager knows better. Mom doesn't understand. Life is different from when she was a teenager. *Everyone* is doing it—whatever *it* happens to be this week. So the child rebels and does *it* against the mother's wishes. Result? He or she gets hurt after making a poor choice. The teenager makes a mistake. However, the consequence of the "mistake" is that he or she learns a lesson. Is it really a mistake if a lesson is truly learned? I don't believe so. After all, why are we on the earth? *To learn!* Mistakes equal lessons. Mistakes are a necessary part of our existence here on earth. Without mistakes we would not learn.

Sometimes the mistakes we make lead us onto another path that is better than the one we were on. I came to Florida at the behest of a man to whom I was once married. We were on a very rocky road in our marriage because of his alcoholism. He decided life would be better in Florida, but after moving there alone, he thought he couldn't live without me and begged me to join him. Against my better judgment and the advice of my irate parents, I sold our condo, quit my job, and arranged to move to Florida. I did all of this based on the promise that he would quit drinking and commit to AA. I naively thought he had finally learned a lesson and would sincerely dedicate himself to sobriety. Therefore, I felt I should give our marriage one last try.

My husband flew to where I was staying and arrived at the door, drunk. The handwriting was on the wall, as they say. Since I had packed up and sold the condo, I had to move out.

Once we were in Florida and settled into an apartment, I found a job. He, on the other hand, was still unemployed after being in Florida a month longer than me. Within one week of setting up our apartment, I gave him an ultimatum. He was unable to live up to his promises, so I booted him out. I had no relatives or friends in Florida and I couldn't afford the apartment alone, so I advertised for a roommate and found a good one. I did everything I could to rectify my so-called mistake, and that included getting a divorce. My parents reminded me regularly that I had been foolish and it was an awful mistake to have moved to Florida.

In the years that followed, I began my studies in mediumship. Eventually I was certified as a medium and ordained as a Spiritualist minister. I became the secretary and then the president of the Cassadaga Spiritualist Camp, and later the pastor of the church, holding each position for four years. I began writing books on spiritual subjects. Along the way I found Vincent, who shared my beliefs, and we married in 1996.

So, was it a mistake to have followed that alcoholic husband to Florida? I don't believe so. If I had not moved to Florida, I wouldn't have had all those wonderful experiences or met my current husband. I probably wouldn't have written several books about paranormal subjects, either. The word "lesson" should be used to replace the word "mistake." Lessons are growth, and they make us better people if we pay attention to the message that is being given to us.

Most of us are a work in progress. Therefore, we do not always conduct ourselves in a spiritual manner. This is because we are "real" people. A real person is defined as one who has foibles, makes mistakes, and most definitely is not perfect. A cuss word might escape from a real person's lips. We get angry sometimes, even though we would prefer not to. A real person isn't a phony goody-two-shoes or someone who tries desperately to project a serene facade that does not reflect his or her inner feelings. A real person is a human being with quirks. We are all on our own spiritual paths, and we should always be aspiring to be better, because that's a good thing. When we aspire to be better, we never stop growing. Spiritual growth is an ongoing process that doesn't end, even when we die. We keep growing on the spirit side as well.

From listening to Marianne Williamson's audio tapes and reading her books, it is easy to draw the conclusion that she fits my definition of a real person. Marianne is a gifted international speaker, an author, and some would call her a spiritual guru. She is the spiritual leader of Renaissance Unity in Warren, Michigan. Prior to her notoriety, she experienced life like any other average female. Marianne held normal jobs—many jobs, actually. She worked in an office, as a cocktail waitress, and she owned a bookstore.

Like many women, Marianne had unresolved issues with her parents and suffered frequently through bad experiences with men. Then she came upon *A Course in Miracles*, which changed her life. *A Course in Miracles* is not a religion, but rather a self-study program of spiritual psychotherapy. It is psychological training in the relinquishment of a thought process based on fear. Marianne has made a career of speaking about the ideas presented in the volumes of *A Course in Miracles*. In her lectures, she teaches how to replace those fear-based thoughts we have all acquired since childhood with a thought system based on love. In each tape Marianne entwines stories about her personal growth as she lectures on topics such as anger, forgiveness, and success. Her tapes are a humorous, wonderful exposure to new healing thoughts. Is Marianne a spiritual lady? I certainly think she is. And she's real.

There are people who have chosen to live a cloistered life. They are sheltered from physical and material temptations, spending time in deep meditation and contemplation. Spiritual communications and inspirations are received, and perhaps delivered to others in lectures intended to guide followers on a spiritual path. People who choose to live such lives are certainly spiritual beings. They serve as worthy examples for us. We should aspire to be like them. With that said, and due respect given, I must say that if you and I were to sit privately in meditation, never exposing ourselves to earthly influences, I believe we could be equally spiritual. When we do not encounter temptation, disagreeable personalities, hateful circumstances, violence, prejudice, and daily stresses, we can easily respond to life in the most spiritual manner. Frankly, I think it would be a simple task to gain spirituality by walling oneself away in meditation inside a temple or seated on top of a mountain. The greater challenge is to grow spiritually living in the real world. If we can successfully do that, we can evolve further in our spiritual endeavors than the monk who never is placed in a position to choose how he will respond to adversity.

As I share my thoughts, personal experiences, and the experiences of others, I hope you will find them helpful in your aspiration to begin a better way to live. Walking a spiritual path is an ongoing journey. It is the process, not reaching the destination, that counts. The process has many avenues, and hopefully this book will help you to find the spiritual path that is perfect for you. Now, on with the journey!

Chapter 2

Beginning the Journey

One of the first things I recommend to people who are seeking to build a spiritual path is to expose themselves to positive influences. What we focus on and surround ourselves with influences us greatly. Books are one means by which to place positive information into our brains. Reading the appropriate material introduces a person to new thoughts, positive behaviors, and suggestions for growth. There is a whole world of information available to the spiritual seeker! The major bookstores have come a long way in recent years, expanding their shelves to offer a wide variety of New Age books. New Age bookstores have also popped up all over our cities, offering books and items that a spiritual seeker may want to purchase. (At the end of this book there is a suggested reading list that is an excellent starting point for spiritually enlightening reading material.)

The reason I suggest that seekers expose themselves to uplifting, spiritual books is because our minds are focused on where we are. If we run around the house or office thinking negative, vindictive thoughts, we are living in negativity. If we jealously hate anyone who achieves more than we do, we are living in negativity. If we blame everyone but ourselves for the path our life has taken, we are living in negativity. But if we actively strive to change our thoughts, we are making attempts to pull out of a negative way of living. When we practice focusing on positive thoughts, gratitude for all circumstances, and loving behavior, we are attempting to live a more spiritual life. And the payoff is that our lives change dramatically.

My favorite phrase is "Just because you think it, doesn't make it so." Change your thought, change your life. What does that mean? When we were children, our parents taught us many lessons. Some of those lessons were fine examples of appropriateness, while others sort of fell into the *wrong* category. For instance, Phil's father was a highly prejudiced man when he was alive. Phil refers to him as the original Archie Bunker because he didn't like any ethnic groups. Apparently he thought everyone should be a WASP (White Anglo-Saxon Protestant). He could spout off a variety of reasons why each culture or race was undesirable. As an adult, Phil discovered that what he had been taught, and thought, was incorrect. *Just because you think it, doesn't make it so.* Phil worked to overcome his prejudice because he felt it had no intellectual foundation. Consequently, he developed many friendships with people of different races during his life who have brought many happy moments and learning experiences. *Change your thought, change your life.*

When we continually worry that something horrible will happen, we are assisting in the manifestation of the worst scenario. "Thoughts are things" is a common expression we hear when participating in spiritual development classes. It sort of goes along with "What you focus on is where you are." Our thoughts are our instruments for success or failure. I once did a reading for a grandmother who constantly worried that her grandchild would fall into the family pool and drown, even though the pool had a safety fence surrounding it. I told her that thoughts are things, and she was giving energy to a situation she did not want to happen. By focusing her worries on the situation, she was actually helping to manifest the worst scenario. Instead, it was better to change her thinking to a more positive frame, such as how lucky the child is to have a pool in which to learn to swim. I suggested to her that every time this worry came upon her, she should automatically give it to God to bless. All she had to do when the worry tapped into her brain was to say, "I give this to God." Therefore, if she started to worry ten times in one day, the child would receive ten blessings instead of ten negative thoughts. By changing her negative thought pattern to a positive one, she was focusing on the positive; therefore, she was projecting a more positive life pattern.

One of the natural laws of the universe is that like attracts like, or, as many of our parents used to say, "Birds of a feather flock together." The term "drinking buddies" means friends who go out and drink together. No one in the group is a teetotaler. People congregate in tobacco shops to smoke cigars. No one in the room is a nonsmoker. A regularly scheduled golf game is attended by associates who play golf. Everyone participating on the green is a golfer. Bowlers in a league are just that, bowlers. They wouldn't be in the league if they couldn't bowl. Each member of a group is attracted to the other because they are similar or share similar interests.

We attract to us people and circumstances that are similar to us in accordance with our tastes and behaviors. When we strive to think in a positive manner and behave similarly, we attract to us situations and people who are also positive. Of course, the opposite is true. Tracy made a habit of hitting all the bars on weekends, looking for men. She repeatedly had less-than-pleasant experiences with the men and concluded from these encounters that all men were bums. A friend told her that if she continued to use the bars as a means to meet men, she would probably continue to find men of the bum caliber. The friend also tactfully suggested that Tracy might want to clean up her own act as well, since she was drinking too much and it was showing in her weight. Tracy was shocked to hear her friend's observation, but it caused her to rethink her life.

After the talk, Tracy decided that maybe bars weren't the best places to find eligible men. She had always loved to read, so she started visiting bookstores more regularly. She joined a book group and became a regular at her local bookstore on Friday evenings, which is when they offered musical entertainment. Tracy found that this was the perfect place for her to meet men who shared a common interest. She began dating a man who owned an antique shop and occasionally gave lectures at the bookstore about owning a small business. Their relationship blossomed because it was built on common interests within positive surroundings, and evolved into a more formal commitment after several months of dating.

By changing her negative behavior to positive behavior and placing herself in positive surroundings, Tracy focused her thoughts in a different direction, which benefited her physically and spiritually. She exposed herself to an environment of learning that brought her a new life. Consequently, she attracted a positive relationship into her life. Birds of a feather flock together!

We can blame everyone but ourselves for our lot in life, or we can accept responsibility for attracting the wrong men or circumstances into our lives. It isn't anyone else's fault but ours. We make the choices. But it's so much easier to blame others, because when we blame others, we do not have to accept responsibility or change. After all, making changes in ourselves takes effort. The easy, lazy way is to do nothing at all and lay the responsibility and blame on others. Someone once said that when we point our finger of blame at another person, three fingers point back at us. How true!

Clarice was a strapping woman. When talking about her, people would often say, "She's so pretty, if she'd just lose weight . . ." She blamed her weight gain on her pregnancies, her children for wanting snack foods, and her husband for demanding that they have meat and potatoes for dinner every night. She did not feel it was her fault that she had gained fifty pounds since her marriage, claiming that this is what happened to all the women in her family. It was a natural course of events. The fault was in her genes.

Clarice was drawn to women friends who were plump or very overweight. One day after hours of shopping, she and her chubby friends went into an ice cream parlor. Each one selected three scoops of her favorite flavor, as was their usual practice after shopping. Halfway through her delicacy, Clarice made an eye-opening observation: her closest friends were fat. Yes, fat. It was an unkind word, but it was the most accurate one to use. She watched as her friends giggled while eating spoonfuls of ice cream that plumped out their cheeks even more. She looked over her shoulder and around the room. Everyone in the shop was fat! There was not one thin person present. The men had stomachs that bowled over their belts, and the women's hips spread across and draped over the edges of the seats. Clarice looked at her dish of ice cream on the table and realized that her children and husband had absolutely nothing to do with her eating this dessert—she had chosen to do so of her own accord. She began to realize that her weight gain was totally her responsibility, not the fault of her family or her genes.

A couple of days later, Clarice made a trip to her local bookstore. She wanted to understand why she was overeating, and figured she could find some answers there. She purchased two books that were intended to help her understand how she attracted this weight to her and what to do about it. From these books she learned that she was an emotional eater, a condition that is very common for women. She was able to analyze her situation and learn how to change her thinking about food and her relationships.

Clarice began to exercise slowly and eat sensibly. She found that it didn't take willpower to resist the snack cakes her children enjoyed. All she had to do was exercise her intelligence. She viewed food in a different light now, so resisting what was unhealthy for her became easy. Clarice lost almost forty pounds in five months, and is still practicing her new life plan. As a result of her weight loss, her three sisters and mother were inspired to evaluate their ample proportions. They also stopped blaming their heredity for their buxom bodies and accepted responsibility for their extra weight. It is amazing how the simple act of changing one's thoughts can eventually manifest into the most pleasant circumstances!

Expose yourself to positive philosophies through books and place yourself in the most positive circumstances possible. *Change your thoughts, change your life.* Negative people and situations bring us down. Positive influences lift us up!

It would be ideal if we could surround ourselves with a peaceful environment all the time. However, we have to be realistic about our spiritual paths, too. None of us live in Utopia or Never-Never Land. We all live where crimes occur, and violence, if not within our immediate vicinity, is certainly easily seen on our TV screens and in the movie theaters. Not too many of us are nuns or spiritual gurus. We have to earn a living and, for most of us, that involves going outside of our homes to work. Therefore, we would have a difficult, if not impossible, time avoiding any exposure to negative circumstances. That's why we have to set boundaries and prepare ourselves for our day.

When we first arise in the morning, we are very receptive to our environment. Our bodies are relaxed and our minds are at peace. When we awaken to the jarring sound of an alarm clock, we are thrown into immediate *go*. It is a shock to our system. Our minds were in a state of peacefulness, then, suddenly, we are wrenched into instant wakefulness. The experience is similar to when you are quietly reading and someone sneaks up on you and says, "Boo!" If you must have a system to awaken you in the mornings, it would be better to have the radio come on with soft music playing. This way you can ease into the morning.

Once awake, many people who are on a spiritual path like to say prayers or meditate. Some write in journals about their dreams or read short passages from inspirational books. By doing these gentle activities first, they are setting the stage, so to speak, for the day. They are starting their new day with positive actions that will help to influence their responses and reactions when less than perfect situations arise. This is a beautiful way to begin the day.

It is not wise read the newspaper or watch the news in the morning. These activities assault our minds with negativity. When there is a media circus covering a famous person's trial broadcasting constantly on TV or war coverage shown repeatedly on every channel, we become saturated with negative information. Sure, at first it's interesting. We want to know why the person did it, if he or she did it, and all the gory details. That curiosity comes with being a human being. The war involves all of us directly or indirectly. Of course we are drawn to the TV screen to watch the coverage. But after a time, we become saturated. Our systems have soaked up all that negative energy like a dry sponge soaks up spilled milk. Yes, we must be informed citizens. But we can do so in smaller doses—and not the very first thing in the morning, please.

Our environment is important to our spiritual growth. It is our responsibility to create a residence of peace so we may attract peacefulness into our lives. A few readers probably rolled their eyes at that statement! You're probably thinking, "Oh, yeah, right. With three kids screaming through the house and the dog yapping at their heels, I'm going to create a peaceful environment? Get real!"

These suggestions are the ideal. It may not be possible to create the ideal in your particular home environment. However, you can, to the best of your circumstances, adjust your environment in some ways that will be more conducive to peace. It's easy to change to a different wake-up device in the morning, avoid the newspaper, and keep the TV set off.

Meditation is an integral part of spiritual growth. It is a practice that even brings health benefits since it helps us deal with stress. Our society lives in a very stressful environment.

We hurriedly awaken in the morning, jump into the shower, throw clothes on, primp, gulp down coffee and maybe some breakfast, and then fly out the door. From that point the stress only builds, especially if we have to drive in rush-hour traffic. Once at work, we are subjected to a barrage of stresses, the degree depending upon what we do for a living. When we return home we are faced with family demands, such as getting little Tammy to her Girl Scout meeting on time and minor crises in the form of little Bobbie's skinned knee or bad report card. It's enough to make one scream! And if you happen to be a single parent, the pressure is worse.

Some women are stay-at-home moms. Their time is spent seeing to the needs of a totally dependent being. The simple act of walking out of a room can lead to an unexpected mishap should the little tyke decide to pull on the lamp cord, causing the lamp to fall on him or her the minute mom's back is turned. How can a mother anticipate everything? The pressure is intense when raising a child.

The time spent in meditation need only be fifteen minutes, but it may be the only peaceful fifteen minutes of the day! The opportunity to relax is essential to our emotional and spiritual well-being, and to our physical health. It is not necessary to meditate for a long period of time to gain benefits. Ten to fifteen minutes is quite acceptable—and you deserve it.

Many folks feel they can't devote any personal time to themselves because it will take away from their responsibilities to their spouse or children. In other words, they feel private time is a selfish indulgence and it makes them feel guilty. Please! It is not selfish to take care of one's self. If that statement wasn't clear enough, let me say it another way: *You must take proper care of yourself in order to be all that you can be for those you love.*

In order to have enough energy and wits about you, you must receive ample rest. In order to be healthy and have enough stamina to get through each day, you must take time to eat. In order to have a sound physical body, you must exercise. In order to keep growing and learning, you must stimulate your brain. In order to experience spiritual growth, you must meditate.

If we want to grow spiritually, we must make a commitment to our enlightenment. This requires that we rearrange our current situations to that end. We have to allow time for meditation and other activities that will help us in our quest. We may have to participate in a physical activity to enhance our development.

Yoga is a wonderful activity to enhance the spiritual quest, and has become increasingly popular over the years. There are a variety of forms of yoga. Currently, a form of yoga that is quite popular is power yoga, probably due to the societal emphasis on becoming healthier and losing weight. Whatever form is chosen, yoga is an excellent practice intended to relax the body, mind, and spirit while focusing on the health of the spine. The principle of yoga is that you are as young as your spine is flexible. It is not a religion, as some people mistakenly think. Yoga is a five-thousand-year-old tradition of physical postures, breathing exercises, and meditation.

While practicing a yoga *asana* (the Sanskrit word for "posture"), the mind becomes more relaxed and present. We are practicing mindfulness. In our busy society, our minds tend to wander and jump all over the place, being too scattered to remain focused for any length of time. This is called the "monkey mind." Yoga helps to focus the mind on the breath, as breath is coordinated with bodily movements when doing each pose; hence, being here now, being present. A gentle *savasana* (meditation) follows the poses, which relaxes the body and mind so we are better able to carry out our daily activities.

The best way to practice yoga is to attend a class. Classes are offered frequently at colleges, in yoga studios, at some YMCA's, and privately. I attend yoga classes three times a week at my local YMCA, and I love it. It adds to the awareness of the body and situations around us. By focusing on the breath, we are forcing ourselves to be present in the moment, a valuable tool in spiritual growth.

Since I started this particular yoga class, which is at 7:15 in the morning, I don't have time to read the newspaper *and* eat breakfast. I was forced to make a choice between the two, and breakfast won. I now find that by the time I return home, I've lost interest in the newspaper and have a stronger desire to get on with my day. Consequently, I've lost interest in the news as a whole. When so inclined, I watch it on TV while cooking dinner. There is no need to bombard myself with all that negativity so early in the morning. To me, this is a much healthier way to approach life.

Yoga videotapes and kits can easily be purchased at discount stores, on the Internet, and through catalogs. A kit usually consists of a sticky mat, foam blocks, and a strap (these items can also be purchased separately).

Tai Chi is another physical way to enhance the benefits of a spiritual practice because it also blends focus with movement, as does working out with weights. Lifting weights requires us to coordinate our breath with movement. All of these forms of exercise will help you to focus, become more aware of your body, and make you present in the here and now.

Here's another suggestion: If you have started walking or jogging to lose weight but find it boring, turn it into a learning experience. Listen to spiritual tapes or CDs on a headset while you walk or jog so that you receive exercise for the body *and* the mind.

It isn't mandatory that you do something physical, but many people find it does enhance their spiritual focus. The choice is yours to make, and I am sure you will choose wisely.

Now you have food for thought and suggestions that will get you started on your spiritual walk!

To-Do List

1. Change alarm to soft wake-up music.

2. Avoid newspapers and news programs in the morning hours.

3. Purchase inspirational reading material, spiritual growth books, and guided meditation tapes or CDs.

4. Vow to begin your day by reading inspirational material the first thing in the morning.

5. Enter a class for physical activity, if this fits your personal tastes.

Chapter 3

Preparing for Meditation

In order to have the most conducive atmosphere for meditation and other spiritual activities, you will need to establish an area in which to create sacred space. Psychologically, when we go to our sacred space to meditate, we feel a sense of reverence because it is our designated place for spiritual practices. It is true that we can effectively meditate elsewhere, but in the beginning, it is helpful to go to an appointed spot. You and any interested family members will conduct your spiritual practices in this sacred space that you create. If no one else in your family is interested in participating, that's fine. It would be illogical and overly optimistic to expect everyone to join you on this new path. Each will come to seek spirituality when he or she is ready. If no one else shares your interest, let this be your special, private area for personal time.

The Perfect Arrangement

The goal is to create a space that is cloistered from the material world so that you can prevent unwanted energies from entering the room. Not everyone has the space to designate one room for spiritual practices. However, if you have grown children who have moved away or are attending college, you may want to consider converting one of the old bedrooms into a meditation room.

Use soft colors to decorate the room, such as blue, lavender, yellow, green, or pink. Loud music and televisions are not to be played in the room. Arguing should not be allowed. No material business should be conducted. If there are windows in the room chosen for your sacred space, so much the better. One wall of my meditation room faces the east, so the sun shines in each morning upon my altar, which is placed in the center of that wall. I have four crystals hanging across the window, suspended from cords, so when the sun shines through, little rainbows dance around the room.

It is desirable to meditate facing the east because this is where the new day begins, suggesting to us that we are starting fresh and renewed from the old. However, it is not mandatory to do so.

Alternative Arrangement

When it is not possible to have a private arrangement, there are alternative measures we can use. Select a room where the fewest number of people will pass through or congregate. Usually the most private area is in the bedroom.

The Altar

When you meditate in your sacred space, it is best to do so in front of an altar. However, if after reading this section you do not feel an altar is suited to your personal tastes, you do not have to create one. You will want to find a table that is made of wood because wood is a natural product. The idea is to be comfortable in a spiritual setting, whatever that means to you personally.

The purpose of the altar is to hold spiritual objects that will remain there between meditations. It is not desirable for other people to handle these objects; they are sacred to you, and another person's personal energy should not be placed on them by touch. Therefore, it is necessary that the altar be located in a quiet room away from the traffic of people.

If you cannot dedicate a separate room for this purpose, it would be logical to place an altar in a bedroom. If you share the bedroom with someone, that's okay. However, you will need to make sure that your partner does not have an objection to an altar being placed in the bedroom. Squeeze a small wooden table into an area of the room. In a loving relationship, there would not be a problem with the other person's personal energy being around your meditation objects. However, he or she still shouldn't handle the objects.

If inserting a table into the room is not possible because the room is too small to accommodate another piece of furniture, then use a portion of the dresser or the night table, for instance. Let this be where you display the materials needed for your meditations. If a curious child's busy little hands are an issue to consider, you will need to keep your special objects in a drawer or box, then bring them out when you meditate. Under these circumstances, you will need to purify (cleanse) the energies left by other people on the night table or dresser by fanning smoke from smudge or sandalwood incense onto your chosen table prior to beginning every meditation. This eliminates other people's personal energy that has been left behind when their belongings are placed on the dresser or table.

Altar Cloth

Most people use an altar cloth to cover the surface of the altar before placing objects on the table; however, it is not mandatory. Those who have to place and then remove objects on the altar may not want to bother with a cloth. If you do wish to use an altar cloth, it should be made of a natural fabric, such as cotton or silk. The cloth may be plain, fancy, or lacy—the choice is yours. White is normally the color used, but there is no reason why pink can't be used if pink happens to be your signature color.

Candles

Candles are an important part of any meditation, in my opinion. Certainly, you could meditate without a candle. For that matter, you could meditate without an altar. Those items are merely fixtures, but they add ambiance and help to set the mood. When we light a candle or change the altar cloth, we are actively, physically, demonstrating our intent. Whenever we add motion to an act, it gives it more power. These accoutrements add so much more to the experience. Candlelight enlivens and beautifies our homes and adds a romantic touch to dinner tables. If you have ever attended a church service in the evening amid the glow of candlelight, you have experienced that special reverence only candlelight can give. In meditation it also creates a sacredness.

Several colored candles can be used during meditation, along with a colored or white altar cloth. It simply depends how important color is to you. For some people, color is everything; for others, white is just fine. The purpose of selecting the most appropriate colored candles or altar cloths is especially important if you are doing a meditation to project a purpose. The phrase "project a purpose" refers to a particular type of meditation that is different from your regular meditation, such as a healing meditation for yourself or someone else, or visualizing a particular outcome to a situation. The color chart on the following page is your reference when selecting the most appropriate colors for meditation. White is always appropriate and can be used consistently in your meditations, or you might want to use a colored candle along with the white. If all you want on your altar is one white candle and some incense, that's fine, too. This is your altar, so you can do whatever you want.

Color Chart

Blue: inspiration, wisdom, peace, tranquility, creativity, and harmony within and without.

Brown: grounding and balance.

Green: prosperity in all matters; healing, balance, and renewal in all areas where growth is needed.

Indigo: creativity, inspiration, and spiritual wisdom.

Orange: puts things in motion, an action color; good for change.

Pink: love, be it spiritual or romantic; spiritual awakening and healing.

Purple: highest spiritual color, protection, inspiration, and spiritual wisdom.

Red: energy, strength, vitality, and passion for life.

White: purity, spirituality, and cleansing; can be used with other colored candles in any meditation to lend additional spirituality.

Yellow or gold: intelligence, the mind, inspiration; useful to bring about change.

Full Altar

If you have dedicated one room for spiritual practices or have a situation where you can leave the altar fully "dressed" in your bedroom, you may decide to have a full altar. In this case you will want to place other objects that have meaning for you on the altar as well. They could be religious or spiritual objects, such as a Buddha, a cross, the Star of David, a statue of Mary, a Quan Yin statue, or a picture of Jesus. This is a highly personal display of what represents sacredness to you.

Crystals or other special stones are examples of items you might want to include on your altar. An incense burner to hold your incense is another item to include. You may add any additional items you desire.

Sometimes uncommon objects that one would hold near and dear are used in a spiritual manner. For example, you could place pictures of deceased loved ones or a container of ashes of a loved one on an altar. The following are items I've included on my altar, just to give you some ideas: soft green altar cloth (square cotton tablecloth); large Asian female statue; Quan Yin; crystal angel; Celtic cross; silver bell to call in the friendly spirits; crystal dish with salt to represent the earth; crystal ball; crystal dish with water representing emotional and spiritual energy; pictures of my mother, father, and maternal grandmother; various crystals and stones; container with ashes of a friend; two candles (colors vary, but usually white and purple); incense burner; candle snuffer.

Ground Rules

Ground rules have to be set once you decide where your private time will be spent. Notice that I said *private* time. The whole point of private time is to be alone and in a place where no one in the family will bother you. Children and spouses will learn to respect your privacy if you are firm in your request. Start by making sure everyone understands that when the door is shut, no one is to bother you. Tell them that if the phone rings, they are to take a message. If someone comes to the front door, they are to say that you are busy. You might want to put a sign on the door to your room that says, Do Not Disturb Unless There's a Fire! Your family will understand and, with a little effort on your part, respect your privacy.

Cleansing

Now that you have created the area for your sacred space, you will need to cleanse the room. If you are fortunate enough to be able to devote one room for this purpose, one cleansing should last quite awhile. However, if you are sharing space, such as a bedroom, you will need to cleanse the room more frequently. If the table area designated for the altar is located in an actively used space, it will be necessary to cleanse the table every time before using it as an altar. This is how to proceed:

Light a white candle, burn incense, and relax your mind with soft music. Close your eyes and take several deep, slow breaths, exhaling slowly. When you feel sufficiently relaxed, take something that will create a lot of noise, such as a spoon and pot or a very loud bell (a cowbell, for example), and walk to the four corners of the room, ringing the bell or banging the pot. Weave through the center of the room, creating as much noise as possible to drive away any heavy, unwanted vibrations. Next, retrace your steps as you swirl the incense in the air. As you do this, say, "I cleanse this space of all negativity."

Return to the chair and close your eyes. Imagine a brilliant white light in front of you. See the light expand until it surrounds you within its bright energy. This is God's white light of love and protection. You are within holy space. Imagine the light growing bigger and bigger, until it fills the entire room. See the white light energy fill every corner, nook, and area within the room. Think to yourself, This room is blessed. Finally, ring a pretty sounding bell, such as the one you would use on your altar, as you walk around the room. This is a welcoming invitation to pleasant, happy energies.

You have just purified your meditation room and made it sacred space!

Remember, if you have just cleansed a room frequented by others, you will need to repeat this action periodically when the area begins to feel heavy following an argument, an unpleasant occurrence, or too much material life creeping in.

Activities in the Sacred Space

Now that you have established an area for your sacred space, there are a variety of activities to enjoy here. Meditation, prayer, journaling, and reading are all activities that are appropriate in your personal space. Some people like to go to their meditation area immediately upon rising in the morning to read a short passage from an inspirational book, like the ones listed in the appendix in the back of this book.

Prayer is one spiritual practice that can be performed in your meditation area. Many people use prayer as their positive projection for beginning the day. After all, prayer is thought. We are placing powerful thoughts into the Universe when we pray to a higher source to relieve someone's pain, grant someone a new job, or fulfill a personal desire of ours.

Another activity to perform in your sacred space is journaling. The purpose of journaling is to create new vision, facilitate healing of the soul, provoke deeper thoughts, and bring resolution to issues. Other activities you may want to record in your journal are your dreams from the night before, and your feelings about what you experience during meditation. The exercises that you will perform later in this book should also be written in the pages of your journal. You will find that journaling is a valuable tool for your spiritual growth.

If time is not limited due to family obligations or intrusions, reading spiritual books for your enlightenment can be done in the peace and quiet of this sacred space also. You may even want to light a candle and burn some incense while you feed your soul through reading.

Meditation

The practice of meditation is the primary reason for establishing sacred space. In meditation you will seek to become more centered, the Balanced Observer. You will also play meditation tapes or CDs while you meditate. To find the best time for you to meditate will probably take some trial and error on your part. Just as one shoe does not fit all feet, one meditation time does not fit everyone. Practice your daily meditation at a time that works best for you. People who are not hampered by time restraints often meditate when they first wake up. This does not mean that you have to meditate when you awaken. It may not be convenient, especially if you have a train to catch at 6 a.m. If you work away from home, the afternoon will not be appropriate either. To meditate directly after dinner is not a good idea for anyone. You will have a tendency to fall asleep or have attention drawn to a full stomach instead of being able to successfully meditate.

I once taught a meditation class for a group of women who worked together. One night they decided to eat an Italian dinner prior to attending class. All through the meditation, much to their embarrassment, their stomachs churned and gurgled, distracting everyone else.

Meditation prior to going to sleep can be a relaxing way to settle in for the night, but some will find they fall asleep during meditation. Eight o'clock at night works beautifully for most people. It is well past dinnertime and not yet bedtime—unless you rise at 3 a.m. to anchor the morning news!

When you have discovered the best time for you, make a commitment to meditate at that time every day. This is important because it shows earnest intent on your part to the Universe. In development circles that commitment is called "keeping a date with spirit." To stress this point, let's use the analogy of friendship. Suppose Jane declares she wants to be your new friend. Jane sets a date to have lunch with you on Monday at noon, but she doesn't show up. She calls to apologize and sets another date for Tuesday at noon. Again, she doesn't show up. She doesn't bother to call and apologize, either. Instead, she calls Wednesday morning to set up another lunch date. With hesitation, you agree to the time. Once again, Jane disappoints you. Are you going to pursue a friendship with Jane? If she breaks promises and can't be responsible enough to show up, how earnest is her desire to be your friend?

Set a time for meditation and stick to it. If you know there is going to be a conflict at some point, such as a child's school recital, simply inform your spirit friends about the conflict during your meditation prior to missing a session, and apologize for not being able to keep your established appointment. Spirit will understand that sometimes life interferes and meditation can't be done at the established time.

The Details

During meditation you should dress in loose fitting clothing so nothing binds your body anywhere. Select a chair that is comfortable, but not so comfortable that you may fall asleep. Some people prefer to sit on the floor, crossing their legs in a yogic fashion with their backs against the wall for support. I don't recommend this position for a beginning meditator because energy needs to flow freely, and crossed legs inhibit the flow. The yogic position is for the more experienced meditator, in my opinion.

In the seated position, arrange your body so that your feet are flat on the floor. Place your hands in your lap with the palms up. This is a receptive pose, and you will be able to feel the energy coming into the palms of your hands. This is because there are small chakras (energy points) in your hands. Close your eyes and listen to a guided meditation tape or CD. These can be purchased at your local discount store or in a music store.

Some people listen to soft music when they meditate, but if you are not an experienced meditator or have a busy mind, you may have difficulty meditating to music. I would strongly suggest that you use a guided meditation, as it gives an active mind something to do. The principle complaint of people who are learning how to meditate is that they can't concentrate and start thinking about other things. A guided meditation is the solution to this problem.

What to Expect

There are different ways to meditate, but all meditation should be a relaxing experience. That's the whole point—to have a few moments of peace. How much further you take your meditation is entirely up to you. The simplest form of meditation is to focus on your breathing while listening to soft music. You direct your attention to how your breath flows in through your nostrils and escapes through your lips. If that's too much at first, breathe in and out through your nose only. When thoughts creep in, gently turn them away, not accepting their presence. Every time you discover your thoughts straying, turn them away and return to concentrating on your breathing. After a few minutes of breathing gently, you may pose a question that needs answering or examine a situation that is causing a problem in your life, as addressed in exercises later in this book.

If you are using a guided meditation tape or CD, the instructor will suggest what you are to imagine during meditation. If you are a novice to meditation, simply follow the instructions as best as you can. The teacher will probably take you on a journey to the beach, mountains, or some other outdoor environment. Usually you are left at some point to meditate in silence.

Don't be surprised if you feel as if you are looking at the back of your eyelids in the beginning. Eventually, this will shift, and you may see a white screen, a colored screen, or colored balls of light. You may also see symbols or images of people and animals, either alive in your material world or from the spirit side of life.

It is important to stress that everyone is an individual and develops in his or her own unique way. The examples I give are considered a common development pattern. There can be no definitive way to describe how you will develop. You may receive on a psychic level, which is a mental ability. Your friend may receive on a mediumistic level, which means he or she is receiving from the spirit world. Later, spirits may communicate with you also. However, it is far more common for people who are just beginning to meditate to receive messages psychically.

Everyone is psychic. Yes . . . you, him, her, and your next-door neighbor. It is a knowing feeling about something happening or about to happen. For instance, suppose a mother senses something is wrong with her son while the child is at school. The phone rings and the mother knows before she picks up the phone that her son's teacher is calling. The teacher tells the mother that little Bobby has fallen and needs to see a doctor. Another example is when we think about someone we haven't seen in awhile, and the very next day we run into him or her at the mall or receive a letter from the person.

Spirits

I have mentioned rather casually that spirits will probably come into your meditations. I hope I haven't alarmed you.

Many people welcome the visitation of spirits because it is through the spirit world that we receive our guidance. If the idea of a spirit appearing in your meditation makes you nervous, let me stress that, out of courtesy, I seriously doubt any spirits will show themselves to you. A spirit's purpose is to guide, direct, and assist you in your spiritual endeavors, not frighten you. Relax, be open, and flow with the impressions you receive. Spirit teachers are emissaries of good, sent by God, Goddess, the Universe. They are meant only to bring you guidance and happiness.

To further explain the possible ways you may receive information during your meditations, let's address the four "clairs."

The ability to see during meditation is called *clairvoyance*. Clairvoyance means "clear seeing" in the language of the French. In rare cases, "seeing" means literally seeing spirits with the physical eyes when we have our eyes wide open. This is objective clairvoyance. It is more common, however, for people to be in a meditative state, viewing images with closed eyes. This is subjective clairvoyance. Colors are usually the first experience beginning students will encounter, followed by symbols, before they experience the image of a spirit, if they ever do. The spirit may appear hazy in form, in full figure, or perhaps only the face or hands will be seen.

Another way to explain subjective clairvoyance is as follows: As you read the previous paragraph, you probably saw images as I described colors or mentioned the face and hands. Your eyes were wide open, but you were "seeing" images.

Whether you see spirits or not, the spirit world is still working with you. Spirits are guiding your development and will communicate with you in whatever manner is best for you and them. They may impress you with symbols, intended for your interpretation, rather than allowing themselves to be seen. Some mediums work strictly with this form of communication and do not see spirits at all, receiving all their impressions from the symbols.

You may receive communication by sound, which would mean you are blessed with *clairaudient* talents. Clairaudience means "clear hearing," which enables you to hear the voices of your spirit guides or other sounds, such as a barking dog or the roar of a plane. Again, these sounds may be very clear and literal, such as hearing music on the radio or the sound of a human voice speaking. However, the subtler sounds are more common. To demonstrate how the subtler sounds appear, it would be similar to thinking how your mother's voice sounds, or the laugh of your baby. You aren't literally hearing these sounds, except in your thoughts.

It is common to hear spirits calling your name at unexpected times outside of meditation. As a developing medium I once had that experience as I lay on the couch watching TV. I heard my name as clear as the proverbial bell, and I was sure I knew who the person was on the other side of the door. When I swung open the door, no one was there. And no one was walking down the hallway either. I never received an explanation for this, so I concluded that the spirit was testing me to see if I would respond.

Another form of communication is *clairsentience,* which means "clear sensing." The best way to explain the meaning of clairsentience is to give the example of attending a community meeting where the city is proposing an assessment against property owners to cover the cost of the expansion of a utility plant. Most of the people are disputing this issue, so the room is full of agitated people. Consequently, the tension in the air feels thick. The vibrations in the room have been disturbed, and disharmony is present. It doesn't feel right.

We could also liken clairsentience to intuition, a gut feeling that something is right or wrong. If we are wise and listen to our intuition, we may find that we narrowly avoid an accident. On the other hand, we could receive an intuitive flash that indicates that what we are doing is correct, despite what everyone else is advising at the time. Something inside just "feels" right about the situation, and you intuitively know it is the correct move.

Clairsentience is also the ability to feel the presence of a spirit. We may feel the spirit standing behind us or beside us. It might feel as if we are being watched from behind, or like an energy is standing close by.

Clairgustance, the French word for "clear smelling," is the ability to smell spirit. Yes, spirits really can emit a scent! Whenever my father is around me, I smell cigarette smoke because this is his way of letting me know he is present.

Spirits frequently will use some form of identification so we can recognize them when they manifest. Since my father smoked when he was alive, he knows that I will realize he is present when I smell smoke. And you know something funny? I have no sense of smell, but I can smell spirits!

Men who are in spirit will normally identify themselves when using clairsentience by impressing us with the scent of tobacco in cigarettes, cigars, or pipes, or by their aftershave lotion. Women in spirit frequently will identify themselves by the scent of their favorite fragrance or flower. If your uncle was a baker when he was on the earth plane, he may impress you with the delicious aroma of one of his favorite baked pastries so you will recognize his presence. If your grandmother used to bake chocolate chip cookies for you because she knew they were your favorite, when she pays a visit you might smell cookies baking.

Since we are all individuals and develop at the perfect pace for our greatest good, please do not criticize yourself if your development does not go quickly enough or you don't "see" something right away. Everything comes when it is supposed to, and not before. Also, we do not necessarily develop all four abilities. If we acquire or enhance two, we are doing great!

From the examples given, you will have some idea of what to anticipate during meditation. It is important to record your meditation experiences in a journal so you will be able to review your progress. When we ask a question for guidance in a situation, sometimes a thought will pop into our minds, the name of a tune, a sound, or we may see a symbol. This may or may not be one of your spirit teachers sending you the answer you are seeking. Jot down your experiences during meditation in your journal. This way, in a few days you will be able to refer back to a particular question and the answer you received. The outcome of the situation or the results of following the guidance should be recorded at that time to see if the answer was correct. In so doing, you will establish an accuracy record.

We can get carried away by interpreting everything that happens as a message from the spirit world. Every time you notice a song persistently in your thoughts, don't immediately jump to the conclusion it is a spirit trying to convey a message. While everything happens for a reason, the "message" you thought you received may also be a figment of your imagination. This is trial and error, and a learning phase. We have to practice to learn how to interpret what we receive. That is why recording experiences in your journal is so important. Upon reflection, your journal will tell you how accurate you are, how you are advancing, and when your imagination is getting the better of you.

To-Do List

1. Buy a journal to record your dreams, meditation experiences, and exercises.

2. Purchase colored candles, incense, and an incense burner, if you so choose.

3. Set aside ten to fifteen minutes daily for meditation.

4. Make time for spiritual reading.

5. Add activities such as yoga to enhance your development, if you wish.

Chapter 4

Affirmations for Your New Life

The powerful effect that words have on us is amazing. If a stranger speaks kindly to us when we are roaming through a department store feeling blue, we blossom. "That's such a pretty dress you have on!" Immediately we brighten after receiving the compliment. It was just what we needed to hear.

On the other hand, when we are the receivers of unkind words, we wilt from the assault. It is common for a couple who frequently argues to say unkind words to each other, swear at each other, and call each other names. When people are in the throes of trying to maintain their position of being right, they can damage other people's emotions, confidence, and well-being by hurling insults at them. Although a spouse may apologize later for what was said in anger, the unkind words are glued to a part of the partner's being. The words are not forgotten and will probably be thrown back at the spouse at a later date. The questions that beg to be answered in the partner's mind after receiving an apology are: "Why did you call me a ___ if you didn't really think I was one? What have I done to cause you to call me that? You wouldn't have said that if you didn't believe it to be true."

One harsh word can cause a person to relive that exchange many times, examining the possible truth behind what was said. This will perpetuate the negative associated with the exchange.

Sometimes people tell mean jokes or make sarcastic remarks that are hurtful. At the beach, a woman who is wearing a bikini shows her girlfriend a bruise on her hip, and her husband says laughingly, "Yeah, if her hips weren't so big, she'd be able to fit through the door!" Of course, he claims he's just kidding. But it makes the wife wonder, Is there truth hidden there? Does he really think my hips are too big?

Words can hurt. But they also have the ability to heal, encourage, and uplift. We would all be wise to choose our words carefully, even during a heated argument, and avoid hurtful, sarcastic remarks.

Since words have the ability to affect us, we can choose to use them to our advantage. Words can help us in our spiritual quest when constructed into affirmations. The definition of the word "affirmation" is "to make a positive declaration." Since it is so important to focus on the positive in our quest for a more spiritual life, the practice of affirming a desire or aspiration is highly beneficial. By focusing on the positive we are attempting to break our bad habits and reprogram ourselves to exhibit an improved habit. For instance, we may want to tone down our impatient, angry outbursts. We may want to look differently at annoying situations or people. Affirmations can assist us greatly in all our aspirations. They help us to attain our goal of being a Balanced Observer.

We have the power to manifest the positive in our lives by viewing written affirmations. The idea is to create a positive statement in writing and then place it where the eyes can read it frequently. These are called *affirmation signs,* and they work beautifully because they are designed to stir the divine spark that is within all of us so that we may create an outward manifestation of our desires. Walt Whitman would probably agree with that concept, or at least that is my interpretation of this excerpt from his poem "There Was a Child Went Forth":

> There was a child went forth every day
> And the first object he looked upon, that object
>   he became
> And that object became part of him for the day
>   or a certain part of the day
> Or for many years of stretching cycles of years.

Whenever you want to bring attention to a particular area of your life, use a computer to create affirmation signs. If you don't have a computer or access to a friend's computer, signs can be created with colored pencils, crayons, magic markers, paint—anything that makes a mark!

For those of you who do have computer access, choose a colorful background from your graphics or print shop program to demonstrate your desires. Select pretty lettering for the words and appropriate colors to coordinate with your desires. For instance, if you were creating an affirmation sign for improved health, it would be best to use green-colored lettering. (Please refer to the color chart located in chapter 3 as a guide for color selections.) The affirmation signs are then placed in conspicuous places around the house, such as on bathroom mirrors or the refrigerator. Then, wherever you go frequently in your home, you will find a reminder to stimulate your subconscious mind into manifesting your desire.

The secret to composing affirmation signs is to make the statements positive and to phrase them as if the situation has already occurred. By inserting the word "now" into the affirmation, we place the aspiration in the present tense. Avoid words like "don't," "never," "won't," and "can't," as they have negative connotations. When these words are combined in a sentence, it reinforces the idea you wish to escape. Examples of some incorrect affirmations would be:

I will never eat chocolate again.

I won't ever swear again.

These affirmations show the use of a negative word, and they reinforce the habit you are trying to eliminate. A better approach would be:

I am now drawn to healthy food.

I only speak kind words.

All spiritual teachers recognize the value of affirmations, and would probably agree that it is preferable to precede affirmations with the words "I am." The "I am" represents the divine spark of God within. By using these words we propel spiritual energy into our wishes, which will flow to the Universe to be manifested into reality. Following are some examples:

I am flowing with the bending trees now.

I am now filled with love for my coworkers.

I am understanding personified.

I am forgiveness personified.

I am a beautiful soul.

I am strong in my convictions for better health.

It is not a mandatory requirement that all of your affirmations be preceded with "I am" in order for them to be effective. The idea is to stimulate the subconscious. If you find it difficult to create a particular affirmation with "I am," simply compose a positive statement phrased in the present. Some examples are:

My senses are opening to Spirit.

God's white light shines all around me now.

I see the spark of God within everyone now.

Goddess blesses every step I now take.

I see before me only bright, new beginnings.

Another tool is to create reminder affirmations. These affirmations are intended to remind us about our desire to improve one of our less-than-positive qualities. One favorite should be "Think nice thoughts." As I said before, thoughts are things. There is energy in our thoughts, and energy never dies. Therefore, when we think positive thoughts, we are building positive energy. Our positive thoughts go out into the Universe and live.

To prove this point, let's look at how numerous people will come up with the same idea at approximately the same time. Someone puts a thought out into the Universe. Perhaps someone else receives inspiration and puts out the same thought. Twelve other people receive inspiration from the previous thoughts floating in the Universe. Six months down the road, suddenly, we have a new trend. All the manufacturers are selling the exact same item. Have you ever had an original idea, then a few months later, or perhaps a year later, you see your idea being marketed to the public?

Our thoughts are powerful. Ugly, hateful thoughts and nasty words spoken in anger travel out into the Universe as well, and *live*. What a frightening thought! All those negative thoughts we have sent out into the Universe over the years about other people are still floating around. All those nasty words we have spoken in anger are living out there somewhere, too. Ouch! So, it's important to watch what we think and say.

Students who are attending classes for psychic development are often told to say "Cancel, cancel" after they catch themselves saying something catty, nasty, or unflattering about someone else. "I hope she gets what's coming to her in my presence. Oops! Cancel, cancel!"

By quickly realizing they shouldn't have said what they did, they attempt to cancel out the damage. They don't want the karma associated with that remark, either. We'll talk about karma in chapter 5.

Reminder signs assist us in instilling a positive thought pattern. They do not have to be fancy; they can be flat statements to instill a positive thought into the mind. Following are some examples:

> *Turn it around to the positive.*
>
> *Think nice thoughts.*
>
> *Flow with events.*
>
> *Speak kind words.*
>
> *Release rigidity to God.*
>
> *Cause no pain.*

You can place several reminder affirmations on one sheet of paper and display the sign on your bathroom mirror. Every time you go into the bathroom, there it is, reminding you of the more positive disposition you wish to cultivate. Other affirmation signs can be placed on the refrigerator door, on the wall behind your computer, or on the dresser. Again, put the affirmation signs where they will be seen frequently.

Periodically, we should change the signs. You will notice at first that the new sign is all you will see, but after awhile it begins to blend into the woodwork, unnoticed. Also, you will require new reminders and affirmations as your life changes. Affirmations and reminder signs should be revolving consistently in order to do their job effectively. After all, we never stop growing.

A friend of mine, Lisa, created a reminder sign with six statements on the sheet of paper. It wasn't too long before a lesson presented itself in her yoga class that would bring her attention to an area needing adjustment. Lisa adores her yoga teacher, Anida, because she feels she is the very best instructor she has ever encountered. However, due to the demands of her full-time job, Anida found it necessary to take one evening off, at least temporarily, so she had a substitute teach the class on Friday nights. Lisa was less than pleased about the change, but figured she would give the new teacher a chance.

The substitute had a totally different approach to yoga, an athletic approach, while Anida taught from a spiritual level. Lisa's greatest concern was that the new instructor led the yoga postures at a hastened pace. It was a regular aerobic workout! Up, down, up again, back down—whoa, this is a killer! Two elderly classmates left in the middle of the class because it was too intense for them. It was too intense for Lisa, too. Consequently, she rebelled and didn't attend for three Fridays.

After Anida announced that the temporary instructor was going to become a permanent teacher on Fridays, Lisa decided to give the other teacher one more try. A more intense workout might be good for burning calories. When Lisa returned to class, the teacher still did everything differently from Anida, and the workout was still more intense, but my friend begrudgingly accepted it. Suddenly, it occurred to Lisa that she was stuck in her rigid mode. She had closed off her positive thinking, rejecting something new. Lisa reflected on some of the messages from her reminder affirmations:

Release rigidity to God.

Flow with events.

She quickly realized that she was only hurting herself when she refused to flow with events and stubbornly closed off her mind, denying the teacher the right to teach as she chose to teach. Lisa went to the class with a more open mind, and returned thereafter. Life presents us with opportunities for growth all the time, in unusual ways, and the lesson for Lisa didn't stop there.

Anida hurt her arm in a fall at work. As a result, she turned over her regular classes to another very competent woman. This new instructor, Jill, had been attending class with Lisa and was known to be well schooled in the practice of yoga. Once again, Lisa was required to adjust and be flexible. However, in this case, Lisa liked Jill, and as a teacher she proved to be excellent! The bonus to this lesson was that the Friday substitute was eventually replaced by Jill. The key is to be open to the lessons when they are presented to us, and perhaps a reward will present itself as a bonus for being flexible! When circumstances change in our lives, we are being given an opportunity to live a new experience. Rather than remaining in the same old, same old, we are expanding our horizons.

Turn it around to the positive.

Flow with events.

If you are a person who needs to tone down angry outbursts, here are some suggestions for affirmation or reminder signs:

I am a peaceful person.

Love flows through me like water down a stream.

How can I see this differently?

Turn it around to the positive.

I am focusing my passionate energy into positive areas now.

I only see the good in people.

For a person experiencing difficulties in several areas of life, here are some examples that may assist you in walking through the pain:

The Universe has a master plan for me.

This situation is for my highest and best good.

Thank you, God, I am learning (or growing).

Behind this door is a new life waiting for me.

I place my trust in God to bring this situation to its brighest resolution.

I am filled with love for all.

To bring more energy into this practice, affirmations can be spoken and chanted. It is a good idea to say the affirmations aloud every time your attention is attracted to the signs. This will place your affirmations into the vibration of sound, projecting even more energy into the manifestation of your desires.

Treasure mapping is another way to attract positive outcomes for your aspirations. A treasure map is a personalized wish list, complete with pictures, objects, and words that will inspire your subconscious to manifest into reality all that it contains every time you look at it. Spend some time in an arts and crafts store or a discount store prior to creating a treasure map. There you will find the basic tools you will need to create a treasure map that will give a power boost to your desires.

Select an ample sized sheet of heavy construction paper, paperboard, or something else you might already have around the house that would be suitable for attaching objects to. Background color is optional. Choose some colorful writing markers or crayons, and pick up some glue. Now you have the basic tools you need to create your treasure map.

People are typically taught to create treasure maps for desires that are more material, such as attaining a new car, house, job, or vacation. But there is no reason why a treasure map can't be created for a spiritual journey as well.

The sheet of paper or cardboard you choose is the foundation on which you will attach pictures from magazines of whatever gives you a sense of spirituality, be it a picture of a cross, a Buddha, a temple, or a tree. Place pictures on the foundation and keep adding bits and pieces as new items come to you. Write words that stimulate your heart to feel love or passages that inspire you. Attach objects to the treasure map that represent spirituality, too.

After it is complete, position the treasure map in a very conspicuous place, such as on the refrigerator or near the bathroom mirror, so that it will frequently be in your line of vision. When you have time, study it at intervals during the day. Let the vision sink into your subconscious mind so that you can bring your desires into reality.

Having done that, if you want to create another treasure map for a material gain, select a picture of your perfect vehicle, most desirable home, greatest career aspiration, or whatever it is that your heart desires. Objects could be included, such as pieces of fabric representing the material you wish to be sewn into your wedding gown, a spatula to signify the cooking school you wish to establish, or a paint brush for your creative genius that has yet to be discovered by the art world. Clip out words from newspapers and magazines to state your goals (for example, Author, Computer Programmer, CEO, Chef, Fashion Designer, Model, or Veterinarian).

A friend of mine who is a writer believes strongly in the power of treasure maps and affirmation signs, and placed his treasure map against the wall beside his computer. Since his map happens to focus on his career as a writer, this placement is very appropriate because he spends so much time at his computer. He has pictures of the covers of his two previously published books glued on the paper, and various inspiring words that he cut from magazines and newspapers, such as Great Writer, Barnes & Noble, Nonfiction, Oprah's Favorite Books, and a list of the top ten bestsellers. He even has a copy of his first royalty check, which he doctored to make it appear like he received a lot more money than he did. That's positive thinking!

Considering how important words and thoughts are, it would be appropriate to mention that other people can sabotage our dreams if we aren't careful. Suppose you wanted to attend a school for acting and submitted a registration application. You anxiously await a reply to see if you will be accepted. One day you share your anticipation with a friend, who promptly tells you that she thinks you aren't good enough to get into the school and that you don't have enough experience in theater to be accepted. This remark trashes your hopes and self-confidence, sending you into a whirlpool of doubt. Now you are working against yourself by thinking negatively about your chances for acceptance. Not only that, but your so-called friend has just sent a lot of negativity about you into the Universe. Her comments, probably motivated by jealously, are reinforced by her negative thoughts.

When something in life is very important to you, it is often wise to "keep it in the silence." Don't share a dream that you are waiting to manifest into reality with other people. You do not need their potentially negative thoughts or words counteracting your positive efforts to bring your dream into reality. People used to think that if they spoke about something before it happened, they might jinx it. That's a bit superstitious, but it has some merit in that we are allowing others to sabotage our dreams by speaking about them aloud. *Keep it in the silence.*

Exercise

Using your journal, at the end of the day write down how many times you:

1. Did not think nice thoughts about someone, something, or a situation.

2. Did not speak kind words to someone, about someone, or about a situation.

After making your list, reflect back on the situations. How could you have changed your thoughts and words around to the positive? Repeat this exercise every night for at least seven days. This will help you to become aware of when you are thinking something unkind about someone or something, and will give you the opportunity to turn it around to the positive at that very moment. This exercise will also help you stifle unkind words before they escape from your mouth and attack another person. (But remember, should you mutter something unkind, say, "Cancel, cancel.")

To-Do List

1. Meditate for ten to fifteen minutes daily.

2. Read inspirational passages upon rising.

3. Create affirmation signs.

4. Create reminder signs.

5. Design a treasure map.

6. Read.

7. Journal your thoughts during meditation.

Chapter 5

Cause No Pain

When on a spiritual path, it is a wise course of action to *cause no pain.* That might sound like an obvious course of action, whether you are on a spiritual mission or just living life—of course we shouldn't cause pain to others! But that phrase has a far deeper meaning.

We have all caused another person, animal, and plant pain at some time in our lives. Actually, it would be quite impossible to look back on our lives and not find evidence of pain we have caused others. Remember your childhood? Reflecting on this period in our lives is the perfect place to find evidence of the pain we have caused. Children are so mean to each other, and that behavior doesn't change, in most cases, when they enter middle school. Girls are known to exhibit aggressive behavior toward other girls who are not as popular; they may send dirty looks, intimidate, gossip, and make threats to those who are in a less powerful position. Boys are not exempt from this brutish behavior, either. We've all heard of the local bully who beats up the smaller kids for not being athletic enough, for being too short, or for looking like a wimp. Any silly excuse will suffice.

How about those teenage years? The situation doesn't improve when youths enter high school. They are either the tormentor or the tormented, and both at different times. If someone isn't popular or "cool," he or she gets teased or tormented.

I remember walking down a long flight of stairs when I was in high school. Two boys were standing near the bottom of the staircase and looked up to see me descending. They criticized the length of my skirt and laughed at me. Apparently they thought the skirt was too long. Their unsolicited opinion should not have mattered to me, but it did because I was a sensitive teenager. I no longer can recall their names, nor do I remember their faces, but I still remember how hurt I was that day. I would hazard a guess that everyone can recall something similar occurring in their younger years.

In our moments of immature adulthood, we continue to cause others pain. Even today, in our jealous moments when we feel threatened, we make snippy comments to the ex-boyfriends or ex-girlfriends of our partners. We make degrading comments about a clerk's lack of intelligence when he or she makes a mistake. We think nothing of chewing out a salesperson in a department store who refuses to take back our merchandise. We scream insults at strangers who cut us off in traffic. Unfortunately, we can't wipe our former actions away like specks off a window. But we can vow to do better—oh, so much better—than we did in the past.

Some people are intentionally mean, hateful, and vindictive as adults, I'm sorry to say. They purposely inflict pain, probably because it makes them feel important or powerful when they do so. Some men take malicious joy in beating their wives. Some women beat their children. People who attack strangers or acquaintances in a parking lot or home are doing so consciously. If these people took the time to think about their actions, they probably would acknowledge that they are mean, and they may even be proud of it.

Some people are cruel to animals. I think it's bad enough to deliberately hurt other people, but to inflict emotional or physical pain on an animal is even worse. Neglect can be as harmful as purposely mistreating an animal. The result is the same—pain. People at least have some hope of protecting themselves. Animals are helpless to our abuse and cruelty.

Sometimes we cause ourselves pain, consciously or unconsciously. We humans are such amazing creatures. We have been given the capacity for so much more than the animals and the plant kingdom. We possess intuition, the potential for wisdom and compassion, the ability to rationalize and contemplate—yet we destroy each other and ourselves. Amazing, the choices we make.

Take the eating disorder anorexia nervosa. A young woman thinks she's too fat, when, in reality, she's painfully thin. Everyone can see how pitifully thin she is, except her. However, this disease is not solely about her physical appearance. It isn't as simple as her desire to become or remain thin. It's all about control and self-image. At some point in this person's life, she has felt unable to control events around her. Whether this stems from dictatorial parents or an inability to cope with life's circumstances, she feels that there is one thing she can be in control of: her body. She can't control circumstances such as the weather or other people, but she can orchestrate how much food enters her body. However, in her attempts to gain some control over her life, she has actually lost control and, in all likelihood, will destroy her life.

Sometimes people cause themselves pain by sabotaging their own success. We've all heard the expression, "You're your own worst enemy." For some reason, certain people feel they do not deserve to be successful, appreciated, recognized, or honored. Low self-esteem is usually the root of the problem. Whatever the cause, they continually hurt their chances for advancement.

Gary was a man of many talents. He was a gifted guitarist and singer, and composed songs that he wished to record one day. Not only was he an excellent musician, he was a natural artist. The oil paintings this man created were absolutely beautiful. His paintings were so lifelike that when people stood looking at a portrait, they would feel they could hold the hand in the painting or that the eyes would blink at any moment.

Gary was truly blessed. But sometimes one's blessing appears to be one's curse. While it was his sensitivity that enabled him to have these abilities, it also caused him to be incapable of handling his own life. Gary was an alcoholic. Some unusual situations occurred during his childhood that probably made him vulnerable to alcoholism. He never succeeded as a musician or as an artist, always doing something, alcohol-induced, that ruined any potential opportunity.

Sometimes we blindly stumble through life causing ourselves pain, not paying any attention to the lessons being handed to us. Consequently, we keep having to repeat the same lessons. One of the most common examples that we have all observed is the propensity of some people to continually become emotionally involved with the wrong people. This attraction works equally well for men and women: women who only date "bad boys," and then wonder why they get hurt; men who only date beautiful, spoiled women, and then wonder why the women leave them. We need to wake up and pay attention to our repeating patterns. These are valuable lessons being presented to us. We can't grow unless we realize that there is a need to do so. If we run around oblivious to patterns that cause us pain, we will keep repeating them. At some point a true friend needs to point out—nicely, of course—that we are failing to recognize the message being delivered, and redelivered.

No one is exempt from causing pain to others. There is a guru in India who goes to extraordinary measures to avoid causing pain to anything, human or otherwise. Two of his followers walk in front of him, sweeping the ground before the guru with leaves so if an ant should happen along the way, his foot will not squash the ant. He doesn't want his steps to cause the ant any pain. The guru knows that there are repercussions for all actions. Those repercussions are called *karma*.

You've heard the phrase, "What goes around, comes around." That's another way of defining karma. When we demonstrate good behavior, good is attracted to us. Remember, like attracts like. Therefore, the opposite is true: when we don't behave appropriately, when we cause another pain, we attract pain to ourselves. All we have to do is pay attention to the outcomes of situations to realize that there are repercussions for our actions. Once we realize that natural law dictates that we will pay for an unkind action toward another, we can begin to monitor our conduct so we do the best we can to avoid accumulating any more karma.

We are required to pay attention, not go mindlessly through life being oblivious to the results of our behaviors. But that takes effort on our part. Someone once stated that ignorance is bliss. Maybe this is true under some conditions, but not under the laws of our government or the law of karma. Under the law of karma, ignorance is no excuse and full knowledge of how karma operates only increases the ramifications. We immediately become more accountable for the choices we make when we know that what we are doing is wrong, according to spiritual teachings, but we choose to do it anyway. Realizing there will be karma to pay for our actions makes the karma we receive worse.

What goes around comes around. What we dole out to others returns to us. When we cause another pain, we will receive pain. When we lie to an individual, we will be lied to. When we gossip about another, someone will gossip about us. When we cheat another, someone will cheat us. The pain may not be returned to us directly from the person we hurt, but it will boomerang at some point in our lives. Once we understand that there are consequences associated with our actions, this lesson can have a great impact on our lives—an impact for the better.

A man named Earl had a hateful personality. He gave every appearance of being on a mission of destruction. Even the way the man walked exuded intimidation and malice. Earl took his negative characteristics and inflicted pain on those he perceived as threatening to him, especially women. Because he loved power, even when he wasn't in a position of power, such as a boss in his employment or an officer of a club, he wielded his weight in an intimidating manner, always pushing to get what he wanted. Since rules seemingly did not apply to him, he delivered vicious verbal attacks to intimidate the weak into doing his bidding. He accomplished this by speaking in such an authoritative way that he actually led some people to believe he knew what he was talking about.

Earl's ego was such that he believed he was always right and that he had all the answers. If a man talked to him about repairing an engine, he knew everything there was to know about the project. If someone discussed their intention to learn to play the guitar, he was a former professional guitarist. Whatever you named, he was the master of it. The only flaw here was that it eventually became obvious to everyone that he really didn't know as much as he thought he did.

Ironically, Earl thought he was very popular with the people surrounding him. The truth was that everyone disliked him intensely, did not trust his mood swings, and some were even frightened of him.

Earl's life eventually took a sweeping detour away from his controlled maneuvering of people. The karma finally caught up with him, because his whole life went into a massive upheaval. He lost his job and then had difficulty keeping one. His new car was a lemon, always in the shop, and his wife threatened to leave him after years of receiving verbal abuse. When she finally gathered the courage to walk out, Earl claimed the ridiculous by accusing her of cheating on him, and he threw her out. Because he had trouble keeping a job and money was in short supply, the bank foreclosed on his house. None of this improved his disposition, of course. Most nights he sat in a bar getting drunk and feeling sorry for himself. Nothing was going right for Earl; his life was rapidly spiraling downward.

Earl could not attract anything nice into his life because he lived by negative standards. While he professed a positive philosophy, he demonstrated the reverse. His mind was closed tighter than a pit bull's jaws to anything that smacked of change or was in opposition to his thinking. To entertain another thought would mean that he was wrong. To admit being wrong would mean Earl's truth was built on a shaky foundation. We can only excuse this behavior by realizing that he is a man who is very insecure, unhappy, and angry.

We have all been in the position of doling out punishment and, on the opposite end of the spectrum, of receiving it in spades. We do reap what we sow, and sometimes in the exact way we dealt the cards. Even when we act against people who have ill intent, who may deserve punishment by any intelligent assessment of the situation, our actions still result in karmic retribution.

Trisha was in a management position at a condominium complex. When she began her job, the complex was in need of repairs and new rules. Many people had been abusing the system, and the previous manager had not been enforcing the rules, so Trisha created rules and regulations that the condo owners were expected to follow. While the new rules would have been considered logical by a reasonable person, they were not perceived so by some of the people living in the condo complex.

A small group rebelled against everything that Trisha attempted to do to improve the structure. In one breath they would complain about peeling paint and an owner's laziness when it came to retrieving his trash cans after garbage pickup. In the next breath they would berate Trisha for assessing a fee to paint the building and for issuing a warning to the negligent trash can owner. Trisha was wrong, no matter what.

Trisha acted in the highest interests of the condo to the best of her ability. Her motto was to do what was best for the whole, not the individual. After all, she had been hired to manage the condo and improve the appearance of the structure. She had even purchased a small condo in the complex, so she was not exempt from the rules she created. But Trisha suffered through many abusive verbal attacks from a select few obstinate people, thus creating enemies because of her dedication to her job.

After approximately eight years, Trisha decided she had had enough discord with that job, so she quit and began working in retail management. Once she was no longer in an authoritative position, she began to receive hateful letters from the new condo manager, who, ironically, had been one of her adversaries when Trisha was the manager of the condominium. The new manager went so far as to make the ridiculous accusation that Trisha had deliberately let her toilet overflow so the condo below her would flood. To make matters worse, it just so happened that the downstairs neighbor had been one of the obstinate people who had caused her so much grief in the past. The neighbor threatened to sue Trisha, but never did.

Trisha's problems didn't end there. She received a nasty letter ordering her to remove her plants from the balcony because she hadn't asked for permission to display them. What was so ludicrous was that her plants had been sitting on the balcony for five years. No one in the condo had ever objected to Trisha's or anyone else's plants sitting on a balcony until she was no longer in a position of authority. They also challenged her right to use a specific trash container, to walk her dog along a certain path, and other supposed infractions.

Trisha eventually gave up the battle. She sold her condo and moved closer to her job. Once she was removed from that environment, she began to see all these events in a new light. She had created karma, and it had boomeranged! Trisha had felt she was protecting the condo from certain ruin, therefore, she had no guilty conscience about anything she had done. She could easily justify her actions as being in the best interests of all. It didn't matter how right she thought she was concerning the decisions she made, her actions still affected other people. If a decision had affected someone else's life, it eventually affected her own. Occasionally she found herself in the same situation others had been in when she was in charge. Trisha learned valuable lessons about the law of karma from that job.

Those of you who already believe in karma may have observed people who appear to get away with everything they do to others. No matter how shallow the act against another, these people merrily live their lives as if everything they do is done with a pure motive. What we perceive to be rotten behavior seemingly has no repercussions.

Sandy is one person who appears to get away with everything. She is an intelligent woman who works as a professional, and has a tendency to flaunt her knowledge and speak in such a manner that one automatically thinks she's an expert. The person in a group who talks the loudest and with the most authority can often persuade others to follow his or her lead. This is Sandy. However, because she is so intelligent she tends to use her knowledge to her own advantage, thus manipulating situations in her favor.

Sandy wielded tricky financial deals that benefited her, bent rules to suit her, charged exorbitant fees, and got away with it all. She was as sweet as sugar until she got what she wanted, and then turned the charm to tart words more sour than pickles. And yet, she didn't plummet into karmic retribution. How do we explain that? How do we explain one person paying dearly for unintentionally causing pain, as Trisha did, while another appears to be given a free ticket after deliberately causing pain?

It is possible that this person is secretly experiencing pain, but we aren't aware of it because we do not know what is happening in this person's life. Many people are private about their affairs, so knowledge of what is happening in their lives may not be apparent to others when we are on the outside looking in. Also, appearances can be deceiving. A person who smiles brightly and projects confidence can easily convince someone else that all is right with the world when, in truth, his or her world is falling apart behind the scenes. We don't know what private torture a person is enduring during the silence of the night. If we did, we just might have more compassion and be more understanding of his or her behavior.

Here's another thought: perhaps the soul isn't intended to experience the repercussions in this lifetime. Maybe the person's purpose on the earth this time around is unique, so whatever karma he or she incurs isn't important enough to be dealt with during this incarnation. Compared to the ultimate purpose of the person's visit to earth or the opportunity he or she is currently being given to grow, retribution pales.

There is also the possibility that what we perceive as being inappropriate and wrong is quite suitable for the circumstances. That's what striving for Balanced Observer status is all about: observing a situation and not placing the title of "bad" or "good" on it. Since we don't know everything there is to know about any given situation, how can we know the underlying details unless we are that person? In a case like this, we have to learn not to be judgmental. We need to learn to see a thing just as it is. There isn't any good or bad, it just *is*. It was never intended for us to place a judgment of right or wrong on a person or situation anyway. That is not our mission as humans. We are on the earth to learn, not judge. Besides, unless we are a Supreme Being, called "God" by some, we are not privy to all the circumstances surrounding any given situation.

Therefore, we can't pass a proper judgment, can we? It's best to not pass judgment on another and simply accept a situation for what it is. *Flow with events.*

To the best of our abilities, let us put into practice the behavior of not harming others. The only outcome we can anticipate when we harm others is that we will be harming ourselves indirectly. Therefore, *cause no pain.*

Exercise

1. Using your journal, write down the name of someone who has caused or is causing you pain.

2. List the many ways this person hurt you.

3. Write down circumstances leading up to the hurt.

4. How do you share in the responsibility of the hurt? Did you retaliate or act in a vengeful manner at any time prior to receiving the hurt?

5. Consider your participation in the events that led to the hurts you incurred. Use your imagination to understand how you think this person might have felt justified in hurting you.

6. Do you see any reactions that would be considered a normal human response?

7. Turn it around to the positive: How have you grown from this experience? What have you learned from your association?

8. What new understanding do you have of yourself?

To-Do List

1. Design an affirmation that is appropriate to your circumstance.

2. Using the same person you listed in the exercise above, do the exercise at the end of chapter 7, "Forgive to Heal."

Chapter 6

I See, You See

How we perceive an event, situation, or issue depends entirely upon the eye of the beholder. As individuals, we see things through the eyes of our conditioning. We do not have the advantage of a helicopter view from high up in the sky that would allow us to see all the events leading up to and affecting a situation and the final outcome. Our scope is limited to our on-the-ground personal experiences and emotions.

What we perceive to be obnoxious behavior (for instance, when we see one individual directing his or her anger at another) may have a deeper meaning. If Earl, who we discussed in chapter 5, inflicts his bad behavior upon George, we would never assume that perhaps Earl is justified in his behavior, because all we see, in our limited scope, is Earl abusing George. We have to consider that maybe Earl is repaying past karma from George, who hurt him in a different lifetime. We don't stop to think that this action is bigger and more far-reaching because we don't have the benefit of knowing about their past lives or personal karmas. We immediately jump to the conclusion that Earl is a mean jerk and poor George doesn't deserve to be treated so poorly. In this lifetime, maybe George doesn't deserve what he is receiving, but in another lifetime . . . now, that's a different story.

It is believed that we incarnate in groups. Families incarnate together, and groups of people incarnate together; for example, villagers from colonial times may reincarnate together in another small town. For all we know, Earl, or anyone else we see acting abusively, may have been severely persecuted in a past life by many others, so Earl is doling out pain to George and his cohorts in this lifetime. He appears to us to be hateful, yet Earl could be demonstrating the cycle of karma. It would pay to remember Earl when we run into someone who is less than amiable to deal with. The behavior we see isn't right or wrong, it just *is*. However, that does not mean we are required to tolerate abusive behavior.

If a woman were to find herself involved in an abusive relationship with someone like our Earl, she should not leap to the conclusion that he is working through some past karma and feel obligated to stay in the relationship and take her punishment. We do not have to tolerate abuse! Such experiences provide us with a lesson so we can grow, since we all grow from our so-called mistakes. Once we have learned the lesson, we can move on with our lives.

The lessons being presented by men such as Earl could be, on a karmic level, that women do not have to tolerate abusive men to be in a relationship, and that they have the inner strength to stand alone and grow into independent women. Since we do not have the benefit of an all-encompassing helicopter view of the situation, we have to trust that everything is in divine order and is as it should be. We simply have to trust that it just *is,* and not judge. However, we could pray for the woman in an abusive relationship to gain strength and wisdom in her situation, and if she asks for our help, we should certainly do all we can to assist her.

Life has interesting ways of uniting us with the best people to teach us lessons. Unfortunately, those people are usually the ones we find the most disagreeable. The woman who gets under your skin at church because she gripes at everyone and criticizes everything: she's your teacher. The man you are dating who is so insecure that he questions your every move: he's your teacher. The woman who acts so superior and delights in making you feel small in public: she's your teacher. The children you are raising who test your patience daily: they are your teachers. The boss who finds fault with everything you do: he's your teacher. These are life lessons being presented to you by the best teachers for the job. *Turn it around to the positive.*

If we didn't need to learn a lesson, we wouldn't be involved with these people. They are present for our highest and best growth. Frequently, once we have learned the lesson, the people disappear from our lives, or else we aren't affected by their actions anymore. We see them for who they really are: people struggling with their own karmic lessons.

When a man or woman displays impatience, anger, jealousy, greed, or some other unflattering tendency, we are able to recognize those characteristics because we hold them inside ourselves. That's sad to say, but it is true. We cannot identify with a particular condition unless we have experienced it. While we could try to imagine what it would be like to deliver a baby from our body, unless we have borne children, we cannot truly understand. We can't understand what it is like to be fired from a job if we have never had that experience. We can never understand why a woman would allow herself to be physically abused unless we have stood in her Manolo Blahniks. Yes, we do have an imagination and can envision what we think it would be like to live through each of these situations, but we cannot truly identify unless we have shared the same experience.

The people who appear in our lives to teach us the important lessons are mirroring us. When we behave jealously because the former girlfriend of our spouse is flirting with him at a party, we are demonstrating our insecurities. Our reaction may be to say unflattering things about the ex, such as, "Margo is so arrogant. She can't say anything nice about anyone. She's so catty!" Ah, who's arrogant? Who's catty? Talk about not saying anything nice! Those were three zingers hurled toward Margo.

While it may be true that Margo is less than kind at times, we all share those qualities, to one degree or another. We don't know why Margo acts as she does. Perhaps she's as insecure as the rest of us, she just doesn't let it show as much. Her conduct is an opportunity for us to learn another lesson and rise above the situation. Once we can understand why we respond to Margo as we do, we can learn to see her differently and perhaps even develop some sympathy for her. When we reach that point, Margo's behavior will no longer affect us.

Perception is a unique faculty, and because we as humans have a tendency to think we know best, our perceptions can be quite askew from another person's view of the same thing. That's why I suggest that we turn it around to the positive.

In a workshop I was teaching, I asked three people how they felt about snakes. One said that she liked snakes, that they were smooth to the touch. Another answered that snakes disgusted her, that they were creepy and slimy. The third woman remarked that there was a clever connotation associated with snakes. Given their feedback, I asked them to consider which interpretation would be correct if they received a snake as a symbol in their meditation in reference to someone? A smooth personality? A creepy, slimy character? Or would they interpret a clever person? Which would be right? All would be correct.

The three perceptions were based on the three individual's personal experiences in life. If one had snakes as pets during childhood, obviously she would have a different perspective than the one who was struck by a snake while walking through tall grass. No one is wrong, everyone is right. It's all perception.

Let's take a black cat as another example. If you saw a black cat during meditation, would this be a sign to you that bad luck is coming—superstitious thinking in some people's minds—or would the cat remind you of your most favorite family pet? Again, your interpretation would depend upon your personal experiences. All symbols cannot have the same meaning for all people. All situations in life cannot be perceived the same way by different people.

It wasn't too long ago that it was considered a "cool" practice to smoke. When I grew up, teenage girls would light up at slumber parties; the parents were unaware of it because they smoked too, and couldn't smell the girls' smoke above their own. Teenage guys and girls smoked as they drove around town in their daddies' cars, attempting to be cool. You were part of the "in" crowd if you smoked, and everyone thought you were so sharp!

When the teenagers grew up, they still smoked because at this point it was considered sophisticated. The movie capital of the world taught us that lesson. Almost every movie demonstrated that Hollywood was having a love affair with nicotine. Humphrey Bogart and Lauren Bacall puffed away on the silver screen, while James Cagney, Bette Davis, Clark Gable, and many other movie stars blew smoke into the air. Hollywood was completely enamored with the cigarette for many years, and even today we see actors and actresses puffing away on cigarettes. No wonder adults smoked back then. Why, *everyone* smoked! You were the oddball if you didn't.

Skip ahead to the current day. Practically no one smokes. It is considered terrible for your health, not to mention the health of others. Smoking is considered to be bad form in restaurants, rude in someone's home, a fire hazard in some places, and illegal in most buildings. Remember when a nonsmoking household would have ashtrays available for smokers? Today a smoker would be told to smoke outside. My, how times have changed. My, how our perception has changed on the issue of smoking.

What would generally be considered a negative, evil, dastardly act committed by one person upon another will have totally different connotations depending upon which group of people we talk to. An excellent example to emphasize this point is the famous "trial of the century" that dominated our television screens for months in the mid-1990s. The trial of football hero O. J. Simpson for allegedly killing his former wife, Nicole, and her friend, Ron Goldman, polarized the white and African-American populations. The majority of the white population thought O. J. was guilty of murder. On the other hand, the African-American population united in defense of O. J. Who was correct in their assessment of this violent crime?

In general, the white population thought the evidence was clearly pointing the finger of guilt at O. J. He had a motive, the access, and the physical ability to commit the act, even with his medical condition of arthritis. Evidence revealed the famous 911 call Nicole made in which she told police that her husband was going to hurt her.

Further evidence showed that O. J. pleaded no contest to spousal abuse charges in 1989. Pictures were shown of Nicole's bruised face in support of that allegation. The white population also cited the famous chase broadcast on TV. O. J. was seen fleeing from authorities in his Ford Bronco. "Why would he run if he were innocent?" they asked.

O. J. is considered one of the greatest running backs in football history. In 1968 he won the Heisman Trophy as the nation's top college football player, and set several National Football League records before retiring in 1979. He was able to capitalize on his fame to become a sports commentator and actor. He was a hero, as well as a role model that the African-American community needed. His accomplishments were something they could aspire to. Children worshiped him, and women adored the handsome man. To the black community, O. J. was a positive representation of what black people could achieve. With so few role models for black people to admire, how dare people try to tear down their idol!

But tear him down they did. They had the infamous bloody glove, the blood-soaked sock at the foot of his bed, and blood samples from his Bronco. The Goldman family blasted O. J. on television. Denise Brown, Nicole's sister, gave blistering accounts of witnessing domestic violence delivered at the hands of O. J. It was clear: O. J. Simpson killed Nicole Brown Simpson, a blond, white woman.

The black community saw this attack on their hero as just another unwarranted assault upon black people. If a white woman hadn't been involved, would such a fuss have been made? And then there was that *N* word. The defense team alleged that Mark Fuhrman may have planted evidence to frame O. J. because Fuhrman was a racist. With a long history of distrusting the police, the black community saw this as another example of abuse of power against their race. Now the whites had committed the unthinkable by attacking a black man with impeccable character, an unquestionable hero. There was no hope for the rest of them if O. J. could be taken down. He was not guilty of murder.

The prosecution believed that jealousy and obsession were the motives for the killings. The belief that the blood evidence could link O. J. directly to the killings gave the white constituency proof that he killed his ex-wife, former football great or not. But O. J.'s defense attorney, Johnny Cochran, and the black constituency saw only lies, planted evidence, a racist police department, and a historical persecution of African Americans by whites who were now out to get O. J.

Hidden somewhere among the diverse beliefs, historical issues, prejudices, and theatrical courtroom scene is the truth, or, to be more accurate, two truths: one, did he or did he not commit murder? And, two, what were the personal truths of the people involved, be they black people or white people? The truth depends on whom we speak to. It's all a matter of perspective.

On September 11, 2001, there was a terrorist attack on the United States. Planes crashed into the World Trade Center in New York City and the Pentagon in Washington, D.C. The Islamic extremists behind the attacks no doubt believed they were correct to hurt the citizens of the United States. The pilots also must have believed strongly in their mission, and considered it an honor to die in this endeavor. Most Americans cannot understand the reasoning behind suicidal attacks against innocent victims.

As human beings, we are all taught from childhood to love our country. Even the wives of soldiers who die in battle are proud to say that their husbands died in defense of their country. America's attackers felt justified in harming us, in killing people, because they considered us an enemy and saw our lifestyle as an affront to their religious beliefs. Our response to the attacks we suffered on September 11 was to retaliate, to get revenge. We humans are a vengeful bunch, you know. Like many other countries before us, we sought revenge on another country, killing citizens as a result of the destruction we created, all in the name of honor, country, and because we were attacked. Who are the terrorists now? I guess it depends upon whose eyes we are looking through, doesn't it? When are we humans, the superior species, going to learn that vengeance against another doesn't work? All we have to do is look to our history books and watch the current news programs for proof that vengeance in any form does not solve the problems of the world.

The mothers, fathers, wives, and children of the family members who were killed due to our bombing of Afghanistan would feel that we are the terrorists. I cannot imagine that their pain from the loss of their loved ones is any less than ours. When the United States kills and destroys in other countries, are we not terrorists in their eyes? Again, it's all a matter of perspective.

If we lost friends and loved ones in the terrorist attacks, we have one perspective of that event: probably horror, hurt, anger, grief, and loss. If no one we knew was lost in the attacks, we have another perspective: most likely shock, outrage, sadness, and perhaps vengeance. If we are Osama bin Laden and his followers, then there is still another perspective: victory. The United States has one perception regarding retaliation: justified. No one is wrong in their perceptions. Everyone is right.

Choice is involved in our actions where karma is concerned. When we think we have been wronged, we can choose not to do something as easily as we can choose to do something. Let's suppose you did something unknowingly that hurt a man at work, and now that he has been promoted to a higher position, he is retaliating against you. You can't understand why this man seems to dislike you. When you gain a better position at work, are you then going to retaliate against him because he hurt you? Before we act, we should step back for a moment and think about the possibility that there is another side to this story. Maybe we should take a moment to think about our reminder signs and insert one of the phrases into our thoughts when we find ourselves involved in situations such as these. Ultimately, it can serve no real purpose to retaliate. *Cause no pain. Speak kind words.*

We should also recognize that we just might share some responsibility, unknowingly or knowingly, in the attack we received from the coworker. For instance, if we unknowingly delayed the coworker's advancement because we didn't do our job fast enough and that affected the coworker's performance, then we unknowingly are responsible. Therefore, we share responsibility for the attack we received. If we, with full intention, perpetuated a rumor that was floating around the office, and perhaps even embellished it, we are directly responsible. Is this person evil because he attacked us? No. He is merely working under a different perception of events—with his limited scope of the situation.

Observe how politicians behave after a presidential election when a new party comes into power. They build themselves up to appear as if they are superior to the previous administration. During their four year period, they emphasize the improvements they have made, according to their party's criteria, and how the former president should have done something different or sooner. Kind words are not often spoken about previous administrations. When it's election time again, and the former party is ousted, the new party begins attacking the previous administration in an effort to paint themselves as superior. It's all a political game, designed to give the public a glowing perception of the new administration. Retaliation. Vengeance. Suddenly, they're the good guys and the other party is being criticized. It just keeps going around and around.

Even when we perceive that a behavior isn't correct, we can choose to do nothing, especially when our emotions are involved. I have a darling cat named Bailey. He is a striped, red fellow, and I absolutely adore him—more than any of the felines I have owned. I find I am much more tolerant of his bad behaviors because of my affection for him. If he clawed something, I would be more forgiving than I would with the other cats. I have a selective perception of Bailey: he's perfect, even when he's misbehaving. He receives unconditional love, always.

At some point we have to make a commitment to pull ourselves into a neutral position so we can see events in our personal lives more clearly. It is necessary that we break the patterns we have allowed ourselves to adopt. We have to ask ourselves: how is what I am doing affecting other people? Am I helping or harming?

Sometimes it's difficult to walk a spiritual path when we are involved in the material world. The decisions we make in business situations, for instance, affect many people inside and outside of a company. Suppose your business profit is down, so you start laying off people, eliminating nonprofitable stores, and changing business procedures. Of course, you feel justified in making these corrections because if you didn't the whole business will be lost. It's a practical move. But the choices you make to salvage the business will also cost many people financially, especially if it results in the loss of their jobs. Is it spiritual to lay off personnel? No. Yet we can't sacrifice the entire company either; that would ultimately affect even more people. The choices are tough to make. Will we suffer karma from our decisions? Probably so. Even though we are taking positive actions that will preserve the company and most people's jobs, some people will still suffer. As I said before, it would be impossible not to cause some pain to others.

There are some people in the world who would rather lose everything they have than hurt another person. A few years ago we heard in the news about a factory that burned down in Massachusetts; hundreds of people suddenly found themselves out of work through no fault of their own. The owner was advised by his financial advisers to collect the insurance money and not rebuild. But this meant all his dedicated workers would permanently lose their jobs. He simply couldn't do that to his people. Instead, the man chose to rebuild his plant. And he didn't stop there. While the plant was being reconstructed, he paid all his workers their full salaries and continued health insurance coverage for all the families. Now, that's an example of a man who made a spiritual choice instead of a material one! His choices harmed no one.

It is very important, key perhaps, to our spiritual growth that we learn to understand the importance of perception in our lives. How we see an issue and how our neighbor may see the same issue could be entirely different—and probably is. It is important to remember that all people will have a different response and reaction to all situations. We each have our own unique perceptions of any given issue. Therefore, when we deal with people who are diametrically opposed to us, it is important to realize that they have their own interpretation and are entitled to perceive something any way they wish, as we are so entitled. We should not retaliate against them because they have done something to us due to their perception of the situation. We must strive to escape the futility of revenge.

There is a saying that advises a person who seeks vengeance to dig two graves—because one will be his or her own. Remember, we are responsible for our actions. *Cause no pain.* Whatever situation you find yourself in, it isn't right or wrong, it just is.

Exercise

1. Take a situation in your life that presently appears to be unfair, or a circumstance that has occurred that makes you angry. Write about it in your journal. Allow all the negative feelings you are holding about this situation to be spewed upon the pages.

2. What events led to your perceptions? Write the events down.

3. Did you play any part in this? Did the effects of your own actions lead to this situation?

4. What could you have done differently?

5. What could other people have done differently?

6. Using your imagination, why do you think people made the decisions they did? Was there vengeance involved? Jealousy? Contempt?

7. Looking through the eyes of the other people, can you understand their truth? Why do you think they felt their actions were justified?

8. What have you learned by going through this situation?

To-Do List

Create an affirmation sign or reminder sign appropriate for the lesson or lessons you learned from this opportunity for growth. For example:

Look beyond appearances.

Unconditional love is in my heart.

Act; don't react.

Chapter 7

Forgive to Heal

When we try to walk a spiritual path, eventually we will be required to forgive those who have harmed us. That does not mean we have to meet with them face to face and tell them that we forgive them for some poor behavior previously directed at us. Actually, that could be an impossible task if the person has moved or died. Besides, this isn't about them at all. They do not have to hear us say, "I forgive you." It is not even necessary that these people know that we have made an effort to forgive them. This act of forgiveness is intended to benefit us in our spiritual development and give us a clearer understanding of the people who harmed us, because it is through understanding that we are able to forgive.

Many situations could be responsible for the need to forgive another. The conclusion of a relationship, regardless of who initiated the breakup, is a time when forgiveness may be in order. We may need to forgive the lover for the behavior that caused us to terminate the relationship, or forgive the lover for rejecting us. Either way, it is an opportunity for personal growth. Losing a job suddenly due to layoffs at work, the severing of a friendship, or our teenage child committing a felony are other times when we may want to seek this form of closure to a situation.

One thing we need to understand is that in all cases of closure, whatever is happening is for our highest and best good. Granted, at the time we may not be able to see any good in the situation, but we will come to that understanding with enough passage of time. The objective is to continually focus on the positives associated with this event. *Turn it around to the positive.* We must trust that the Universe will unfold a deeper meaning for this experience and lead us through this portal into a new awareness of ourselves.

Forgiveness is often in order when it comes to a divorce. With divorce being so prevalent in our country, many of us should be forgiving the antics of our former spouses. If you divorced a spouse years ago, but are still harboring major feelings of animosity, it would benefit you immensely to spew your ugly feelings into your journal, then practice forgiveness. Those emotions need to be healed, the grief cleansed away, even if it is years later.

If you are currently in the throes of reaching a settlement for possessions, custody, support, and visitation rights, journaling can be a great benefit. This is the perfect way to release the pent up anger and hostile emotions that are fermenting within. We must remember that even though a spouse may be acting like a jerk through the divorce process, or has behaved so in the past, that doesn't give us license to behave that way. Rise above, don't lower yourself, and your children will respect you, if there are children involved. If your spouse has behaved badly, the children realize that. Don't follow the example. *Cause no pain.*

Journal your emotions until genuine forgiveness is possible. Safely pour into your journal all the ugliness and nasty feelings dwelling inside. It is never too early to start. By the time the divorce decree is signed, you could be rid of most of that negativity. This procedure will also help you to maintain a calmer demeanor when you are in the presence of your spouse. Remember, this will also benefit your children. Witnessing one parent being hostile to the other or overwrought because of the spouse will not help your children adjust to the divorce.

The whole point is to create a healthier, happier attitude about the divorce, and manifest that perception into reality. The truth is, the past cannot be changed. It is what it is, period. No amount of hate, vengeance, or tears will wash away the past and make it okay. Hating anyone for something he or she has done only serves to perpetuate a negative situation in our lives. It is far better to accept that an event has transpired in our life that was less than favorable, and move on. By not releasing the situation, we are holding on to it and reliving it daily. The worst possible result of this practice can be illness.

After divorcing their father, Beth began raising her three children alone. Although her ex-husband had manipulated her during their marriage, the primary reason for the breakup was that he sexually molested their oldest child. Beth had no forgiveness in her heart for her ex-husband. She considered him lower than sand at the bottom of the ocean.

Years after the divorce, this man still appeared to have a hold on Beth's life. She was unable to bear going through the possessions her ex-husband had left in the shed, and she even refused to hire someone else to haul the stuff to the junkyard. The ex's possessions were a constant reminder that she had not moved on with her life. While her previous husband had remarried, twelve years after the divorce Beth was still unwed—she wasn't even dating.

Frequently, she would grumble about his late child payments or having to take him to court once again to claim what was owed. Beth cursed his existence and vented her hatred over her ex-husband, yet refused to move on with her life. When it was suggested that she needed to forgive her ex-husband's behavior—not condone it, but forgive his mistakes in order to heal herself—she refused. It appeared she had plenty of energy when it came to playing the role of martyr, and far less when it came to actually doing something about her situation. Apparently she preferred to live in the past, where hurt dwelled.

Certainly, no good can come from this refusal to release pain. No amount of animosity will heal the pain nor banish it to oblivion. Even if we are just going through the motions of forgiveness at this time due to extreme circumstances in a former marriage, we will feel lighter and relieved of a portion of the burden we are carrying. We can always repeat the exercise to forgive at a later date. Eventually, the pain will dissipate, and one day we will fully and completely forgive.

We may have friends who have betrayed us in some manner. There may have been situations in which a boss or coworker mistreated us, lied to us, or in some way hurt us intentionally. However difficult it may be to forgive transgressions against us, that is exactly what we must accomplish in our minds and eventually within our hearts. In the forgiveness of another, our soul, our spirit, is released from the bondage of contempt and set free to explore higher realities.

It would also be wise to forgive ourselves for causing another person pain. We should attempt to reach a personal understanding of why we acted in a manner that inflicted pain on another person. If we are making an effort to understand our family members, friends, or others who have hurt us, we certainly should exercise some understanding of ourselves as well. It is equally important to forgive our own misbehaviors. After all, our past behaviors were a result of our former perceptions. *Change your thought, change your life.* Our former selves have taken a new path and have changed from what they once were. We are not the same person anymore. Carrying around a mound of guilt about a former self is not a healthy practice. It is important to remember that forgiveness benefits our spiritual and physical bodies, besides affecting our mental outlook. It helps us push forward into our new spirituality. So, forgive yourself, too.

Every person who offends us has an outer shell that we recognize as a body. The body houses an inner being that is a perfect spirit. Even when evidence is to the contrary, it is important to remember that everyone, *everyone,* has a beautiful soul. Perverted and abusive behaviors are unconscionable and do not hold any redeeming value, but nevertheless, we must focus on the positive lessons presented to us rather than the horrible demonstrations we were shown. Good is born from so-called bad. As difficult as it may be, eventually we must reach a level of forgiveness for those who have demonstrated what we perceive to be unforgivable acts.

If you have experienced an aberrant act and forgiveness seems impossible, try seeking a new understanding. You can consciously choose to view any situation in your life through different eyes. That doesn't mean you are required to agree with the behavior, it simply means you can see it differently, through understanding. In the movie adaptation of the Pulitzer Prize-winning novel *To Kill a Mockingbird,* Atticus Finch tells his daughter, Scout, that you can never really understand a person until you consider things from his point of view; until you climb inside his skin and walk around in it. With passage of time, true forgiveness is possible for all of us to accomplish through understanding.

A young woman of seventeen was beaten so badly that her mother could only recognize her feet. The girl's boyfriend was killed in the random assault. Every bone in the young woman's face was broken, she lost an eye, couldn't speak, and required seventy-five stitches in her skull. After two surgeries on her eye, two on her face, and one surgery on her nose, she entered physical therapy.

At first her reaction to her situation was anger. She locked herself in her bedroom because she didn't want to be around anyone. Later, when she allowed herself to be more social, she was so bitter that her friends soon grew weary of being around her. Finally, becoming tired of being miserable and angry, the woman decided that she had the power to change how she felt. Acknowledging that she really did want people around her and desired to be loved, she realized that she wasn't going to receive what she truly wanted by continuing to be angry and bitter. She came to realize that her attacker was human and had made a huge mistake. Since she had survived the attack, she believed that God had given her a second chance, so why not give her attacker a second chance?

Now, at the age of twenty-eight, if her attacker were to be released from prison, she would be comfortable with that outcome. Consequently, the woman chose to forgive her assailant, and feels that by doing so she became the hero of her own life.

It isn't easy to forgive someone who has committed an act so heinous. But if someone involved in such a horrific event has the strength to do so, we should be able to forgive our transgressors for the more minor issues.

Sometimes we are asked to forgive a stranger who has harmed someone we dearly love. Understanding the circumstances surrounding this individual can bring about feelings of forgiveness, even for heinous acts. A compelling story is one in which a woman's twenty-one-year-old son was shot in the heart. As a result, the mother suffered through years of hate. Finally, no longer able to live in her self-created bubble of anger because it was destroying her, the mother agreed to a speaking engagement at the same prison that held her son's murderer.

The mother planned to really "let the inmates have it," but during her talk, she saw a young man with bright red hair who resembled her deceased son. A thought crossed her mind: what would the mother of that redheaded boy want her to say to her son? What could she say that would help him turn his life around?

Afterward, the mother decided to meet her son's murderer, and she forgave him, which brought the man to tears. As a result of this meeting, she tried to help him turn his life around. Now they exchange letters and he considers her a mother figure because he never received love from his own mother. Through understanding, we are able to forgive.

Children sometimes suffer verbal abuse at the hands of their parents or relatives, and many women carry around unwanted baggage regarding their mothers for years, harboring resentments about the treatment they received from their mothers. This emotional damage needs to be washed away so we can learn to understand our mothers more fully. It does not serve our spiritual growth to hang on to negative emotions regarding either one of our parents. If you have not released old baggage from your younger years, you may wish to purge some "junk" by doing a little emotional housecleaning. Journaling is highly beneficial when it comes to purging the garbage we have stored in our hearts and minds over the years. Short of going to a psychiatrist, journaling and letter-writing exercises are the best methods in which to achieve this release. We may shed some tears on this journey, but they will certainly be tears that cleanse and uplift our spirituality.

In many cases, parents, relatives, or friends do not know they have hurt us. If we suffered in silence, how would they know? John never knew that by calling his daughter stupid he was hurting her self-esteem. She was too young to voice that to him, and he was only following patterns he had learned from his parents. John did not deliberately set out to cause his daughter pain. His intentions were honorable; it was the method he chose that was incorrect.

If we recognize that parents or friends are probably unaware of the pain they have caused, then it is easy to see that it is fruitless to hold on to our anger, hurt, and resentment. It serves absolutely no valid purpose. For heaven's sake, they don't even know we are upset! Forty years hence, why would they? We are only causing ourselves anguish and possibly ill health by clinging to past abuses. But if we forgive our abusers and release that pain, they can't hurt us anymore. When we see through different eyes, we see the truth, and the truth doesn't hurt.

Frequently, the punishments we were dealt during childhood were learned by our parents from their parents. Sometimes, to understand our parents, we need to reflect back on the personalities and economic circumstances of both sets of our grandparents. If we can understand the upbringing our parents experienced, then we can better understand what made them the way they are. Even if people have similar backgrounds, they may still interpret what they experienced in totally different ways.

Helen and Joan grew up during the Great Depression. They both experienced hard times during their childhoods, but as adults they had completely different attitudes regarding money. Helen never wanted to live by pinching pennies again. Although she was a believer in saving money, Helen purchased the best clothes, furniture, handbags, and shoes she could afford. Joan, on the other hand, became very frugal as an adult, and always looked for a bargain or purchased the cheapest item she could find. To this day, she pinches her pennies until they scream.

Once Joan's son Jack realized the circumstances in which his mother grew up, he was better able to understand why she had insisted on him wearing hand-me-down clothes to school. Joan wasn't trying to embarrass or punish him, as he had thought during his childhood; she was merely mimicking her frugal upbringing.

Knowing the background of any individual helps us to understand his or her behavior. Through understanding we can forgive behaviors that we found objectionable in the past.

A man named Rick was abused as a child. His father, Tom, beat him, but never touched anyone else in the family. Rick was often beaten black-and-blue for little or no reason at all. Affection was in short supply in the household. Years later, Rick became a very charming, handsome man. He sought love, affection, approval, and respect from everybody—especially women.

Rick had a steady succession of girlfriends, exchanging one for another repeatedly. One could have used the expression "Love 'em and leave 'em Rick" when referring to him. He had problems with his self-esteem and suffered from depression, so he drank to alleviate the pain. Eventually, he lost his job due to alcoholism, which led him to seek help in a rehabilitation center. It isn't difficult to understand why Rick developed the behaviors he did. One need only look at his childhood to understand why he hurt people, albeit unintentionally.

We must seek to forgive those who hurt us. We are not hurting them by holding on to our anger with a Herculean grip—we are only hurting ourselves. In many cases, our offenders don't even know or can't remember hurting us, especially if the hurt occurred many years ago, say, at the hands of a school bully. They have completely forgotten the events that caused us pain. Life has gone on. The only one still clinging to the hurt is us.

If someone from our past hurt us deliberately, with all due intention, we must still forgive that person. Why? Again . . . because it heals *us*. The same basic principles are at work here: Learn about the previous conditioning the person was exposed to in order to gain an understanding of his or her behavior. So, does that mean we have to forgive the unforgivable? Yes. We must forgive those who have harmed us so we may heal our spirits.

A minister, his wife, and their two children were sitting down to eat dinner when a stranger knocked on their door asking for directions. The minister let the man inside before he realized that the intruder had a gun. Next, an accomplice entered the house with a shotgun. The two men forced the minister, the wife, and the son to lie down on the floor. They were promptly bound by their hands and feet.

Soon the two men discovered the twelve-year-old daughter and ordered her to remove her clothes. Both men raped the young girl, tied her up like the rest of the family, then sat down at the table to eat the family's dinner. Once they finished eating, they shot the parents several times, killing both. The brother and sister were also shot, but survived the attack.

The two men were eventually apprehended and sentenced. One was given life in prison, and the other received the death penalty. Years later, the brother and sister attended the execution of the man who had been sentenced to death. The rape victim thought she would receive closure after seeing the execution of her assailant, but it didn't happen. Rather, her impression was that the executed murderer got off easy because all he received was a needle in his arm, while her parents experienced terror before they were killed, as did she during the brutal rape. It seemed like an unfair punishment. The woman, consequently, received no peace of mind from watching the execution, and her anger continued.

What turned the woman around was observing people who reacted with bitterness and became hardhearted over minor issues—nothing close to the terror she had experienced. She started to forgive and let go. While it was not an excuse for their behavior, she realized that the two men did not have the advantages as children that she had as a child, and were drunk and on drugs at the time of the attacks. The woman knew that at least she had the freedom to let go, and from that point, she was liberated from her pain.

There's a phrase in the Bible that says, "Vengeance is mine, sayeth the Lord." We should leave vengeance to God, or whatever higher being we believe in, rather than take things into our own hands. We don't need the karma that comes along with vengeance. That which flies back at people who are vengeful is not pretty.

Divorce Forgiveness Exercise

During the divorce process and after, whenever you encounter your former mate, it is best to focus on that perfect inner soul so you will manifest a speedy healing. Try thinking the following sentence repeatedly while in the presence of your ex or soon-to-be-ex-spouse: I see only your beautiful soul. It may sound like a corny thing to do, but try it. You will feel the difference immediately inside your spirit.

Write in your journal the emotions you are still holding on to about your ex or soon-to-be-ex-spouse that are not for your highest and best good. Do this after meditation. Express any feelings of betrayal, hurt, abandonment, or guilt—whatever is appropriate in your particular situation. The purpose here is to use the vehicle of the written word to release any ill will or guilt you may feel in your heart so you may step forward as a renewed, enlightened person. Take as long as is necessary to accomplish this release process. In the next day or two, answer the following questions:

1. What kind of a person is my spouse/ex-spouse? ("Jerk" is not an appropriate answer. Be honest.)

2. What is important to him or her?

3. Did he or she have aspirations during our marriage?

4. Were all his or her desires realized, or did he or she feel cheated?

5. Was he or she happy during the marriage?

6. Were there money problems during the marriage? Did his or her parents have financial difficulties when he or she was growing up?

7. What kind of a relationship did my spouse have with his or her parents as a child? What is the relationship like now?

8. Did I experience treatment from my spouse that he or she might have been exposed to as a youth? Could conditioning from his or her childhood explain my treatment?

9. Was my spouse mentally ill or a substance abusers? What about his or her parents?

In your journal, write down any realizations you received about your former spouse.

For a few days, contemplate the issue during meditation. After three days (but no later than one week) of deliberating, create a letter of forgiveness in your journal, even if the words are not truly felt yet. Focus the letter, in a positive way, on words of forgiveness for whatever transgressions you feel he or she inflicted on you. For example:

> *I forgive you for not listening to me. I know you did not realize how important it was for me to be heard by you.*

> *I forgive you for being insensitive to my needs. Given your childhood, you probably reacted as you were programmed to react.*

Finally, send him or her off with the hope he or she will eventually find self-understanding and grow from having participated in the marriage. For example:

> *It is my desire that you will come to realize how to be a person who is sensitive to the needs of others.*

> *I wish for you to become an attentive listener and develop the understanding that people need to be heard.*

Sign and date the letter, but *do not mail it.* Thereafter, if you start to resent your new situation or are frustrated by your previous spouse's continued loutish behavior, you may feel supported by reading this letter. Also, do not think or speak negative words about this person anymore. If you catch yourself rolling backward and verbally trashing your ex-spouse, say "Cancel, cancel." *Think nice thoughts. Speak kind words.*

Parent or Relative Forgiveness Exercise

After meditation, write in your journal the resentments, hostility, feelings of neglect, or any other emotions you carry about your parent or relative. Get it all out of your emotional system. The next time you meditate, write down the answers to the following questions in your journal:

1. What kind of a person was my parent/relative when I was a child?

2. What was important to this person?

3. Did he or she have aspirations when I was a child?

4. Were all his or her desires realized, or did he or she feel cheated?

5. Did he or she appear to be happy?

6. What kind of a relationship did my parents have when I was a child? Did they love each other?

7. What was their relationship with their parents or grandparents like?

8. Did my parents treat me as they were treated by their parents as a child? Could there have been reasons why I was treated as I was?

9. Was anyone mentally ill or a substance abuser?

When you have completed the questions, take out your journal and write about the realizations that came to you. In the future, should you feel the need to bolster your self-esteem or revisit the issue for a clearer understanding, it will be very healing to read about the things you gleaned from doing this exercise.

Think about the results of this exercise for three to seven days. Then, in your journal, write a letter of forgiveness to the offending parent or relative when you feel moved to do so. Make it as heartfelt as possible. You may want to state how that person hurt you, what his or her actions did to you, and how angry you are about the whole situation. Let yourself feel whatever emotions come to you. Then state that he or she is forgiven. Say something like:

> *I forgive you for the harm you caused me due to your conditioning (illness, lack of self-esteem, whatever you feel caused the situation to occur). I now realize you did the best you could with the information you possessed at that time.*

Close with a loving thought, such as:

> *I know you loved me, even though you were afraid to show me how much.*

> *Despite your rigid behavior, I know now that you were looking out for my best interests.*

> *I love you anyway.*

Sign and date your letter, but *do not tear the letter out of the journal!* This is not a letter intended to be mailed; this is your healing letter. Read it occasionally to reinforce your understanding. Avoid saying or thinking negative words thereafter about your parents or relatives. If you slip, say "Cancel, cancel."

General Exercise

In your journal, write down the name of the person who hurt you.

1. With your new understanding, begin to write a letter of forgiveness to this person. Take as long as you want.

2. Say a prayer, blessing this person to his or her highest and best.

This exercise can be used to forgive anyone who has harmed you in some manner at work, at school, in the gym, during a rehearsal of a play—whatever the case. In the future, when you feel the need to forgive someone, reread chapter 5 and do this exercise.

Chapter 8

Understanding Disappointment

Catastrophes know no season
We'd banish every earthquake,
Despair, and tragic heartbreak.
Since catastrophes know no season,
Perhaps it's ours to reason.
Hearts marked with woes a'clinging
Ought hark to song and singing.

—Anonymous

There are times in our lives when we feel the Universe has thrown us a curve ball. What our hearts yearned for the most, what was once our desired outcome, did not manifest as we had intended. Whether we experience a disappointment on a minor level or one of a colossal magnitude, it hurts.

All week long, sixteen-year-old Allison had eagerly waited for Saturday night to arrive because her favorite musical group would be performing at the local arena. She had wanted to attend this concert for several years, and her boyfriend, Jason, said he could get tickets. When Saturday afternoon arrived, Jason appeared at the front door, unexpectedly. He sat down with Allison and explained how he had expected to purchase tickets at a discount, and then the deal had fallen through. Now, it was too late to even buy tickets at full price. They could not attend the concert. Allison was devastated. While logically she realized that this was not the end of the world, she felt strong anger and disappointment. She continued to be miserable for several days.

A business folding, an engagement broken, or a gold medal lost in competition are certainly devastating events of a higher magnitude. Physically, we often feel empty and numb when large disappointments rock our worlds. Our thoughts are scattered to the four winds, and time creeps by seemingly at the pace of the slowest snail on earth. We may suffer through stages of grief that are similar to experiencing a death in the family. It is common to have feelings of shock, denial, anger, and sorrow. After all, we have experienced the death of a dream. Woe is me, poor me, we think. Life just isn't fair.

With all that said, our destiny may lead us to a place that is entirely different from where we thought we'd be. Let's take John as our example. He had planned to be a doctor ever since the fourth grade, and had applied to certain universities during his senior year in high school with that goal in mind. But John was not accepted at any of the schools he wanted to attend, so, feeling highly disappointed, he decided to attend a local college. Once in the throes of college life, where boundless opportunities are presented, he discovered a love for photography and moviemaking. John decided to be a media major, no longer having the desire to be a doctor. The thrill John experienced when behind the camera could not begin to compare with the image he had of himself as a doctor diagnosing patients. The very idea now sounded boring. He was delighted to be in a field that presented new adventures and challenges whenever he began a different project.

When we are in the initial stages of a major disappointment, it is very difficult to throw off those hurt feelings and say, "Oh, everything will work out fine. I just wasn't meant to win." Can you imagine Michelle Kwan saying those words after she lost the gold medal at the 2002 Olympics? For years this girl set her heart on Olympic gold, only to come home with bronze. Some achievements have a once-in-a-lifetime window of opportunity. There are no second chances or additional opportunities for redemption. Such was the case for Michelle Kwan.

When met with a challenge of this magnitude, we have to dig deep inside to recover. Platitudes fall deaf upon our ears when offered as consolation. There are simply no words that can relieve the hurt or change the outcome. It just isn't going to be right, at least not in the way we interpret the word "right."

All one can do under circumstances like these is to allow time for recovery. Be angry, mope around, cry—do whatever you feel led to do until you feel like doing something productive. Some very wise person said that time heals all wounds. How true! A week after a devastating disappointment, the pain will have lessened—not vanished—but it will exist to a lesser degree. A month later, the hurt will be far more tolerable, and so on. Often, we feel better when we allow enough time to pass.

We have all experienced disappointments in our lives, and we have survived. We can survive whatever it is that we are going through in the present or anything that arises in the future, too. It can be very helpful to reflect back to a time when we experienced a blow to our intended plans, and then think about where we are today: happy, despite the past events.

Molly was engaged to be married to a young man whom she had met at college. They had spent four years together studying and falling in love. A December wedding was planned after graduation. One week prior to the wedding date, Molly's fiancé decided he was too young to get married. He wanted to bike through Europe and explore the Rocky Mountains before he settled into domestic life, say, when he was thirty years old. Molly was understandably crushed. It took six months of grief to heal her broken heart, not to mention her embarrassment. Now, at the age of forty-five, she looks back on that period in her life as a growth experience. Whenever she is confronted with a small or large disappointment, she thinks about that trying time. If she could survive that, she figures she can survive anything. (Today, Molly is happily married to an orthopedic surgeon and lives in a lovely home in San Francisco.)

Often when we use the reflection method to help us heal, we soon realize that the current disappointment is not as grave as the one from the past. Even if it is a severe disappointment, we are reminded that we have the strength to endure such calamities. We have learned that these disappointing events have mysterious ways of working out for the best. Certainly, we can't see that when we are in the middle of our devastation. But because we know that things always work out for the best, this current situation, too, shall lead us to our highest and best. Since we don't know what our highest and best is yet, we are asked to trust in the process, knowing that the Universe has a plan for us.

When one door closes, another opens. In the cases I have shared, each person reinvented his or her life. John had to choose a different college, which led him to a totally different field of work. The new career choice John made was just as valid as his first choice. However, if he had been accepted into any of his chosen colleges, he would not have been exposed to the media arts, which led him to a vocation that gives him such satisfaction. Molly had to change her direction also. Instead of becoming a wife at that particular time in her life, she became employed. Through her employment she met the man she would marry, who provided her with a very comfortable lifestyle. The man Molly married was certainly equal to the first man she was engaged to, even superior in some areas. If she had married the first man, she would have experienced life with a spouse who eventually would develop a gambling problem.

During the recovery time of a disappointment, try to recognize what is positive in your life. In your journal, make a list of your good qualities, the many talents that you have, the material things that surround you, and any other situation that is of a positive nature. For instance:

> *My health is great and I am physically in good shape because I exercise.*
>
> *I am an educated person with a good career ahead of me.*
>
> *The apartment/house I live in is adequate to my needs at this time.*
>
> *My vehicle provides decent transportation.*
>
> *I live in a great city with many activities.*
>
> *I have parents and friends who love me.*

At the end of your list, write: Everything is in Divine Order. Your life really is progressing as it should, even though you may wonder if God has forgotten you. No, you are not forgotten during disappointing times. Quite the opposite is true. The Universe provides equal amounts of love, opportunity, happiness, and abundance for every person. It may not appear to be that way from our limited perspective, but it's true. Our abundant moment may simply be scheduled for a later date. *Flow with events.*

Sometimes it is wise to allow circumstances to lead us to where we are meant to be. This takes some effort on our parts to be aware of our lives, what's happening, and how events are unfolding. A friend of mine named William wanted to be a full-time writer. He had had moderate success with his writing, but during one period of time, assignments were nonexistent. While William had mailed out several proposals for a column and a book, his inspirations were not being accepted.

William was concerned that he might have to abandon his writing to get a steady job so he could continue to pay his bills. He began looking in the classified ads for full-time jobs, but found that he wasn't qualified for what was available. Next, he contacted friends for leads on part-time employment, which would at least allow him time to write, but nothing manifested there either. With each passing day, he grew more and more worried.

William mailed another proposal to a publisher, and a another idea for a column to a newspaper. Just when he was convinced he wasn't meant to be a writer, the dam broke. A publisher contacted him about his book proposal, the newest column idea was accepted by the newspaper, and he was offered a part-time job. William suddenly found himself busy trying to fulfill all his obligations, much to his delight. The floodgates opened and prosperity washed over him.

Apparently William was not meant to hold a regular, full-time job because one never came about. His first ideas for a book and column were not accepted, then he came upon the last two inspirations, which attracted interest. The part-time job was a necessary financial filler for William, arriving at the perfect time. Looking back, William understood why things had happened as they did. He realized he should have flowed with events, knowing his highest and best would come to him at the appointed time.

Spiritual law teaches us that we are setting ourselves up for disappointment when we allow ourselves to "expect." When we place our expectation upon a controversial approval turning in our favor, a situation working out the way we think it should, or an event happening when we want it to, we are setting ourselves up for failure and disappointment. God has not given us any guarantees that we will be granted whatever we want, even if we pray for it to manifest. That's simply not how life works. What we need to do is practice being a neutral observer of life, not expecting things to work the way we think they should from our limited viewpoint. We are asked to release our attachment to a particular outcome and surrender the results.

When we realize that everything is truly in Divine Order, we are able to let go. In other words, we give it to God to handle. Therefore, we are relieved of the burden of our current problem. The Universe has a plan, a better one than the one we have imagined. Flow with events so that the plan can manifest without interference. It's much less stressful that way.

Jane was a talented musician who worked in a record store for several years, eventually earning the position of assistant manager. When a new manager was brought in from outside of that particular chain store to fill a vacancy, life became unbearable because of the new demands and rules set down by the manager. It appeared that the new style of management was intended to dislodge Jane from her position. She drew the conclusion that the new manager felt threatened by her knowledge and experience. When she finally objected to procedures, she was fired by the new manager.

Jane reeled over the insult and loss of her career with the company. Her goal had been to rise to a managerial position within one of the company's stores some day, and now her chances were ruined. Heartbroken, she sulked around her apartment for weeks, not knowing what to do next. She didn't just lose a job, she lost her career. Where was she to turn now? It would be awhile before she would realize that the new manager had actually done her a favor by firing her.

Jane's husband suggested that she view this as an opportunity to write music and market the songs, a desire she had carried in her heart since childhood. For weeks Jane sat at her piano, tinkering with the keyboard. Nothing happened. Then, one day, inspiration plucked her heartstrings. The notes, the lyrics, everything came rushing into her brain and fingers. Jane was composing! After six months of disciplined work, she began to send tapes to some friends she had acquired through the music store who happened to work for a music industry mogul. She received positive feedback, and was directed to submit a resume to a company looking for music for TV ads. Due to the generous reference from the music company, she was contracted to write three "jingles." She was on her way!

Jane wrote music for another year, and submitted more material to the music company. The response this time was even more gratifying. The company wrote that they would send the tapes to several singers whom they thought would be appropriate for her music. Several months later, Jane was notified that two of her songs had been selected for CDs. She had sold her music and established a rapport with a big music company—a dream come true!

If Jane had not been fired from her job, she never would have had the time necessary to compose music, her life-long dream. Her expectation had been to become a store manager; however, the Universe had a bigger, better plan for her.

It seems we are most inclined to reach out to God for support when we think life has turned on us. We have a tendency to avoid talking to God when everything is going right. But let our private world cave in on us and, suddenly, we want God to help us out of the avalanche. And that's okay; we're humans, after all. During times when we are experiencing disappointment in our lives, prayer can be very beneficial to transport us from hurt to healing. Prayer is the means used to establish dialogue with whatever we recognize as our higher spiritual being. We find comfort in this exchange, or else we wouldn't seek the communication. Even if we do not literally hear comforting words, we hear our words being delivered, and there is healing in that practice. If you have been practicing meditation, you should have already established some type of communication with your intuition, and possibly feel from sensing that you have been in touch with a higher being.

Pray before your altar or on the floor beside your bed—kneeling or standing upright—it doesn't matter. Wherever you are comfortable is where you should pray. When desperate for spiritual comfort, we can pray while walking or driving our cars. Sometimes we pray constantly. God hears all prayers; it doesn't matter where they are given. You might try the following prayer to assist in your transition:

> Mother, Father, God, please comfort me in my time of need. Let me feel your embrace that I may know that you are with me. Surround me with a peace that will remove this hurt from my body, heart, and mind. Open my eyes that I may see what the message is in this lesson. Tell me how I am to proceed in a way that I cannot help but recognize and understand. Help me to accept that this has happened for my highest and best good, for I know God is limitless and at work here. Life works in mysterious ways, and I know that You are in charge at this time in my life. I trust in the process and know that

everything is in Divine Order and is as it should be. I open my arms to receive Your wondrous blessings now. And so it is.

Let go and let God work the magic in your life. Let the Universe shoulder the burden now; you've walked under its weight long enough. Whatever is ahead of you is intended for your highest and best spiritual development. We are all children of God, and God only wants what all parents desire for their offspring: happiness. Everyone faces disappointments in life. No one is exempt. But we children do grow up and learn to understand the lessons given to us. As adults, we must also grow through our experiences and learn to trust in the process. If we have managed to endure harsh times in the past, we certainly are capable of sustaining ourselves through whatever obstacles are thrown on our paths now. This, too, shall pass, and we will be stronger, wiser, and more sensitive to other's needs because of this new encounter. Thank you, God, I'm growing!

Exercise

1. Think back to your teenage years and remember some disappointments that you thought were devastating at the time. You survived, didn't you?

2. Reflect on disappointments during your adult years that were devastating to you at the time they happened. List them now in your journal, and write the final positive outcomes in your journal. Can you see, in retro-

spect, how everything had a way of working out for the best? If you had but known then how things would turn out, would you have reacted so severely?

3. How can you take the lessons from yesterday and use them in the present? Write your thoughts in your journal.

4. Are there things that you do to set yourself up for disappointments? In your journal, list any behaviors that come to mind.

5. What steps can you take to change this behavior? Write ideas in your journal.

To-Do List

1. Create an affirmation sign that will help you to avoid disappointments in the future.

Chapter 9

Unconditional Gratitude

To ask someone to practice gratitude might sound like a silly suggestion. Everyone is grateful when nice things happen. Who wouldn't be delighted and grateful to receive a present? Who wouldn't enjoy a night out at the movies? How about receiving a new car? We're certainly filled with gratitude every time we receive a raise or promotion! But our goal is to be grateful when not-so-nice things happen. Perhaps you think that's an unrealistic goal, and wonder to yourself, Who could possibly be grateful for lousy occurrences? Well, every one of us should strive to be grateful, because those so-called lousy occurrences help us to grow, learn, and become better people.

We always have two choices when presented with a situation that is less than desirable: we can make the best of the situation or make the worst of it. Some people would probably declare that they would rather not go through the lousy stuff, thank you very much, and just remain as they are, not growing if it means experiencing painful things. However, no matter how we feel about it, we all will receive our share of growth experiences, whether we like it or not. Regardless of how we respond to a bad situation, the experience is happening anyway. We are not in a position to change circumstances such as being fired from a job or getting a divorce. It's right there in our faces, and it isn't going to disappear. We might as well make the best of it, don't you think?

Our only other alternative is to wallow in the situation, groan to all of our friends, exist in an angry state of mind, and ignore the lessons presented to us for our growth, but if we do, we won't evolve beyond where we currently find ourselves. Our friends are going to grow very tired of all that moaning and groaning, and we will gain nothing from trying to get their sympathy. Being enshrouded in sympathy only stalls our development. It forms a shield around us that prevents us from venturing forward because it reinforces our "pity party."

Those tough life experiences are intended to be our growth lessons, and they are important to all of us, especially those of us who are consciously seeking to walk a spiritual path. If we are aware, we can recognize those situations that are intended as opportunities for our spiritual growth. Our attitude should be to accept what life deals out with open arms, and say, "Thank you, God, I'm growing!" Yes, that is a very idealistic perspective. However, it's also a very positive way to view any situation presented to us for our spiritual growth. Our goal is to choose to take advantage of this opportunity to grow. *Turn it around to the positive.*

We all know people who resist growth. How many times have we seen someone repeat the same experience, over and over, until we think, Why don't they get it? The pattern is obvious to us as we observe a friend's behavior. Why can't they see their errors? we wonder.

Repeat patterns are frequently seen in the area of our love life. Countless times women have come for readings because of their messed-up love lives. They just can't find the right guy, they lament. Instead of Mr. Right, they attract Mr. Wrong—different face, same scenario.

A client of mine, Amy, complained that all the men she dated eventually turned out to be abusive jerks. They drank too much, cursed a lot, and eventually became abusive. Amy would end the relationship when she felt her safety was in jeopardy, vowing never to date anyone like that again.

The next man on the scene would appear to be nice, charming . . . and strictly a social drinker. But after a while of steady dating, the alter personality would rear its ugly head. Amy would then find herself contending with a drunk passed out on her couch, with a cigarette dangling from his fingers, the burning ash threatening her carpet and sofa. When she would state her concerns to the man, he would become defensive and hostile. Amy would forgive the first incident, and probably the second. Thereafter, it would become a regular event, always ending with the man yelling unkind remarks at Amy, sometimes roughly grabbing her arms and yelling into her face. "Why does this keep happening?" she asked.

We have an intuition, especially if we are women. That intuition usually warns us about situations that could turn ugly. We get a "feeling" inside, a notification that something is wrong. I asked Amy if, upon meeting a new man, she ever felt a familiar sensation inside that made her think, Here we go again? Amy said, "Yes." She understood what I meant. Something inside would warn her that a guy had a strong potential to be like the other abusive drunks she had dated. I asked her why she continued the relationship once she had that feeling? She said it was because she thought maybe things would be different this time. After all, what were the chances that this man would be like all the rest? Surely, he *had* to be different.

Amy is an excellent example of how we refuse to pay attention to the lessons that are presented to us for our highest growth experience. Rather than make a change in ourselves, we choose to remain in a life-rut. Consequently, we develop a pattern of behavior, and then we wonder how in the world this can keep happening to us. There's no "wonder" about it. We created the behavior and are choosing to remain trapped in this self-destructive pattern, resisting our potential for growth.

I told Amy that in order to break out of this pattern of behavior, she had to stop dating men she instinctively knew would hurt her. When she received the first hint from her intuition that the new guy was like all the men from her past, she needed to turn around, run in the other direction, and put an immediate stop to the relationship. If she gets this feeling on the first date, so be it. If she feels it at the first introduction, so be it. Run the other way! If she didn't do this, I advised, she would continually attract men of the same caliber.

I asked Amy to dedicate time to some self-discovery so she could understand why she attracted abusive men to her. You see, Amy was a nice lady; she was attractive, a little shy, and held a position in a company that provided her with many financial comforts. She was not deliberately placing herself into situations where she would be exposed to men who had the potential for abusive treatment, and wasn't doing anything consciously to attract this type of man to her. I advised her to relax to some soft music and contemplate this issue, answering two key questions: (1) on some level, did she think she deserved abusive treatment? and (2) when growing up, was she abused, or was she exposed to others being abused, such as her siblings or her mother?

If she answered these questions honestly, she would gain an understanding of why she attracted this sort of man. Once she understood, Amy could break the cycle. In the meantime, Amy needed to be grateful for this opportunity to grow, and she needed to create affirmation signs for improved self-esteem.

Growth has only positive connotations associated with it. Expressing a phrase such as "Thank you, God, I'm learning" is sending a message into the Universe saying that we understand and accept this growth experience, and we *turn it around to the positive*. We are stating that we are aware that this experience is for our highest and best good. Although we may not understand all the ramifications of what we are going through at the time, it will become apparent later.

Doug was experiencing a lonely period in his life after his girlfriend abruptly ended their two-year relationship. To add insult to injury, his boss decided that the last man hired was the first man fired when his business went into a slump. Doug was the last man hired. Depressed and alone, he sat in his apartment, lamenting his life. No job, no girlfriend, and no life, as far as he was concerned.

A close friend, realizing Doug's situation, decided to step in to help ward off any further progression of this problem. Bill advised Doug to journal his feelings. Doug, being a macho kind of guy, thought it was a bit effeminate for a man to be journaling feelings. Bill, being a former college basketball player, told Doug to slam-dunk that way of thinking. If Doug wanted to get over his depression, he needed to work on himself.

Following Bill's instructions, Doug began to journal his feelings daily for one week. First, he poured out his anger, hurt, and any animosity he felt toward his former girlfriend. Next, he listed the ways he felt he had been treated unfairly at work. Doug poured out the anger he felt toward his boss on the pages, and the frustration he felt over having to find another job. After each daily entry into the journal, he would close with the phrase "Thank you, God, I'm growing." Doug didn't understand what he was growing into or what he was supposed to be learning from this situation, but he trusted that something good would rise from the damage. After a few days of spewing his venom over the hurtful way his girlfriend ended the relationship and the unfairness he felt about losing his job, Doug began to feel his negative emotions depleting. He was still sad and lonely, but his anger was definitely subsiding. After the week ended, he was relieved of his anger completely.

Trust was an important component in the process. Through the journaling exercises, Doug remembered experiencing other break-ups in his past relationships, and the fact that he had healed after a while. He knew, logically, that he would heal again and would eventually meet someone new, as he had before. Doug also realized through this week of journaling that he had lost other jobs and had always found a new one, which was usually better than the former. He realized that this would be the outcome this time, too. It would only take time. By reflecting back on other situations that were less-than-pleasant, he recognized that he would get through this, too, and be better for the experience, as he always had been before. He was learning to trust in the process.

Three weeks after being fired from his job, Doug acquired a position that offered more opportunity for advancement. Comparing the former job with the new one, he also realized that his boss had done him a giant favor. Doug had not been content with the lack of advancement opportunities at the former job, and had considered seeking employment elsewhere. But that process took time and effort, and Doug felt it was easier to stay where he was. When his boss fired him, Doug was forced to find another, better job. *Thank you, God!*

Sometimes the Universe has creative ways of shaking up our world when we become stagnant. If we don't keep growing, the Universe pulls the rug of life out from under our feet that are so firmly planted in our complacent lives.

Doug's love life didn't improve quickly, but this gave him time to reflect on some of the problems that led to the ending of the former relationships. He listed the problem areas in his journal, and also noted what he wanted in a relationship. The next time Doug met a woman, he vowed to get to know her better before jumping hastily into a committed relationship, as he had done before.

We seem to learn our best lessons when there are unpleasant circumstances surrounding the event. If all our events were pleasant ones, we wouldn't pay much attention to them, taking everything for granted. However, let something unpleasant happen, and we suddenly appreciate the former pleasantness. If we didn't have so-called bad things happening in our lives, we wouldn't be able to appreciate the good things that happen. When we are hurt, experiencing disappointment, treated unfairly, or suffer from grief, we pay keen attention to the lesson being delivered. Most of the time, good comes from bad. And that's why we use the term "so-called bad." If we learned a valuable lesson and our lives were improved, how was that a "bad" experience? Although it may have been a painful encounter, good did eventually manifest from so-called bad.

We must strive to recognize that when life throws us a ball covered in greasy dilemmas, this is another opportunity to grow. We must trust in the process that this really is for our highest and best good, and believe that the Universe does have a divine plan all worked out for us, although we may not understand what that plan is at the moment. And how could we? We don't have all the pieces to the puzzle yet. We don't know what the Universe has in store for us in the future. But we must trust that it will be better than what we have now. *Flow with events.*

How many times have we been involved in relationships that failed? We've all been there, some of us more than others. Can't we all look into our pasts and remember when we were devastated beyond belief over a breakup? Perhaps we thought this person was the perfect one for us, that no one else could ever match this individual in charm, looks, position, or whatever. We are totally torn apart over this awful turn of events. Now flash forward to the present, where, say, you have a wonderful spouse and three darling children. Where is that love of the past—and do you really care? Not likely!

Many of you can look back and agree that you are so very glad it didn't work out between you and your ex because your life would not have turned out as you had anticipated it would back then. At the time, you were looking through the proverbial rose-colored glasses. You didn't see this person for who he or she really was. Your present life is so much better than it would have been should you have stayed with that first individual. Things work out for the best. No matter what situation you find yourself in now, always keep this in mind.

Reflecting back on past situations helps us to heal in our present circumstances. It shows us that we must have faith that everything will work out for the best this time, too, because it did previously. The Universe has a plan for all of us. Give it a little time and the Universe will manifest a new beginning—a bright, beautiful awakening.

Sarah Ban Breathnach wrote a wonderful book called *Simple Abundance*. In it she talks about the importance of expressing gratitude. Sara suggests that every night we list five things for which we are grateful. In doing so we learn to appreciate the small things in our lives and also recognize how blessed we really are. We gain an appreciation for all the wonderful things, people, and situations in our lives, no matter how big or small they may be. We also gain an expansion of our blessings by showing our gratitude for them. By expressing gratitude, we are focusing our positive attention on areas of our lives. Gratitude is a thought, and *thoughts are things*. This goes back to my first remarks in this book: when we focus our attention on something, we are giving it energy. We are helping to bring into manifestation whatever we focus on. Like attracts like. We give thanks for our job, and we receive a raise. We give thanks for our small house, and a larger, newer house becomes available for purchase when we desire one—at the perfect price and within our budget. We give thanks for our family unit living together, and we become more closely attuned to each other. When we express gratitude, we are following a positive action: focusing on abundance rather than lack. Therefore, by expressing gratitude, we are giving energy to something, thus it will attract a positive and expand.

By expressing gratitude for what we currently have in our lives, we are also recognizing simple things. Every day cannot be a bonus day. We do not receive raises and promotions constantly or find a golden opportunity to purchase something at a discounted price. Sometimes we are asked to appreciate the norm, the simple things, like our comfortable bed, a nice dinner, or sandals with enough life left in them to be worn through another summer. We are gaining an appreciation for the simple things in life. And there's certainly nothing wrong with that.

Sometimes gratitude is found in our gardens. Beauty in nature can certainly awaken our senses to the joys of simplicity. We take so much for granted! What if an oil tanker spilled some of its cargo into the ocean near your home? The next time you idly walked the newly oil-stained beach, you would be shocked to see dead fish along the shoreline or pelicans covered in oil. Your appreciation for the formerly pristine condition of the beach would suddenly grow. Don't let it be necessary for a lesson of this magnitude to appear in order to jolt you into a grateful state of being. Express gratitude for all that surrounds your wonderful world *now*. You live an abundant existence already, today. Tomorrow may bring better things to you, but right now is wonderful also. Appreciate what you have and express your gratitude. Your abundance will multiply.

We are energy. Our thoughts and actions also carry energy. Therefore, when we are in motion, we are moving energy around. You may not have given any thought to the concept that when we spend currency, we are also spreading energy. It is a positive practice to distribute the abundance we have received. Now, that does not mean it is wise to spend our money foolishly! What I am suggesting is that we should not hold on to our money with a closed fist. Imagine that your money is like whipped cream. If you tightly close your fist, the whipped cream oozes out between your fingers and the sides of your palm. But if you open an empty hand, more and more whipped cream, or money, can be heaped into your hand.

Some people would have us believe that money is evil and we should not seek to acquire it. I would ask you to consider logically how money can be evil. Money has no soul, intelligence, or thought processes, and can't make a decision. Money can't do anything of its own accord. So, how did it warrant a decree of evil? We humans are the ones who place a decree of good or bad on something. Money doesn't have a connotation of good or evil. It is an inanimate object, and as such it cannot make us behave as greedy people or contaminate us so we become dissatisfied with what we possess. We come to that personal choice of our own free will. Money cannot create those human characteristics. Therefore, money just *is*.

We should express our gratitude for the abundance we attract to us as a result of demonstrating gratitude for the simple things in our lives. When our abundance increases, we should share our prosperity. Money, when used appropriately, can be a healer. Money, combined with love, can be nourishment. Money, given generously, can be someone's salvation. The idea is to keep the energy flow moving.

One spiritual law is that we cannot add to something that is full. For instance, if you had a cup of water, you could not add more water to the cup unless you emptied some of the liquid contents. So, in order to invite new items to flow into your life, besides expressing gratitude for what you currently have, you should remove the extra "stuff" to make room to receive. When money or objects flow out of our hands, they will also flow back in. We reap what we sow, in other words. We have to give to receive.

If you need to purchase some new clothes for the office, but can't seem to find anything appropriate, pack up the clothes you have outgrown or become tired of and donate them to a charitable organization. This is spiritual recycling. The items you wish to add to your wardrobe, such as new shoes or a suit, will soon become plentiful or go on sale. Stashing away older clothes in the back of the closet until they come back in style or until you return to a smaller size benefits no one. That's a closed fist with oozy whipped cream seeping out.

When we are prosperous, we should share with others who are less fortunate. Should a time come when we are not prosperous, we will want to be the recipients of another's generosity. If we have not been generous, we will not receive, either. In other words, what goes around, comes around. You never know when you will be on the opposite end of that energy flow and require assistance.

A friend of mine usually purchases 14K gold or silver jewelry. Sometimes she grows tired of the same earrings or simply doesn't find them appealing anymore. Being a believer in keeping energy flowing, she recycles her jewelry. One Christmas she came up with the bright idea to mail her cousin and her cousin's two daughters a package filled with her discarded gold and silver jewelry. All three women were delighted to receive this generous treasure! My friend kept the prosperity energy moving by recycling her jewelry to others. What a wonderful idea!

We also should express our gratitude for the opportunity to give. Good fortune has smiled upon us and made it possible to share our abundance with others. I am always impressed when wealthy, famous people donate large sums of money for a good cause, such as when Stephen King and his wife Tabitha made a donation to the library in Bangor,

Maine. That is an excellent example of how we can spread positive energy that will help many people. Who knows how a child may be affected by this generous act? Perhaps he or she will discover a cure for a cancer. Never underestimate the power of one. One person can save your life by performing an operation. One act of kindness can melt a cold heart and transform a person into a warm human being. One small gesture can make a lonely child feel welcome among strangers. One smile can bring joy to an elderly widow in a shopping mall. Ah, the power of one—and that one could be you.

To-Do List

1. Take some time during your next meditation period to list in your journal all the events that have occurred, people you've met, places you've visited, accomplishments you've achieved, possessions you've acquired, and all your wonderful characteristics for which you are grateful. The list should be sizable. Try for one hundred things, at least.

2. Express gratitude daily when you journal or meditate.

3. Gratitude can be expressed in any environment. Express gratitude as you drive to work. Be grateful for a safe journey, or be grateful when traffic moves steadily along and there are no accidents delaying your arrival to work or your arrival home.

4. When stuck in rush-hour traffic, say aloud what you are grateful for. In other words, count your blessings. Expressing your blessings aloud in the car gives you something to do while you wait for traffic to clear.

5. When at the tail end of a checkout line at a discount store, count your blessings.

6. Express your feelings of gratitude to your family and friends. Everyone likes to be acknowledged.

7. Make a treasure map or an affirmation sign for gratitude. Suggestions for affirmations are as follows:

I am entitled to prosperity, and I give thanks for my abundance now.

God blesses my every endeavor.

I am grateful for my health, wealth, and happiness now.

Prosperity is my entitlement.

I am blessed with prosperity in every area of my life.

I give my prosperity to God to manifest now.

May God's will be done.

Chapter 10

Prayer

We pray for many things we wish to achieve, gain, occur, and sometimes not occur, in our lives. Prayer is a positive activity that can bring forth, or, at the very least, encourage, the manifestation of an outcome. Frequently, we express our desires through the deliverance of prayers, directing them for the benefit of individuals whom we care about. We pray that our children make good grades. We pray that a parent recover quickly from surgery. We pray that a spouse's medical test results are negative of disease. We pray that a friend is hired at a particular new job. We pray that our teenage daughter returns home safely from a date. If we do all this praying, we certainly must believe that it has the potential to create a positive outcome.

Even the medical profession, historically short on belief in anything miraculous, is coming around to recognizing the effectiveness of prayer. An article that appeared on WebMD Medical News November 6, 2001, titled "People

Who Are Prayed for Fare Better," stated that prayer works, even if medical science can't explain it. One study showed that people who were prayed for by a prayer group prior to having cardiovascular surgery had fewer complications during and after surgery than those who were not prayed for. Each prayer group was assigned the name, age, and particular illness or condition of a patient for whom they were to pray. It did not matter whether the group doing the praying knew the patients, what religious persuasion the prayer groups were involved in, or where they were located. Results were still realized.

Patients at an in vitro fertilization clinic in Seoul, Korea, had higher pregnancy rates even when total strangers prayed for them to conceive. The study showed that women who were prayed for doubled their chances for conception over the ones who were not prayed for. This very controlled study left the medical community baffled over the results. The doctors readily admitted that they didn't know what the positive results from prayer meant.

WESH TV in Orlando, Florida, ran a news story in March 2002 about the benefits of prayer resulting from experiments at Duke University in 2001. In one experiment, people were asked to pray for only 50 of the 150 heart patients who participated in the experiment. Those fifty who received prayers responded the best to treatments. Prayer apparently made the difference.

Numerous family members were interviewed at Florida Hospital in Orlando, Florida. They were asked if prayer had assisted in the recovery of any of their family members. A mother whose child had received four surgeries expressed her belief that prayers had carried her boy through all the surgeries. Others also agreed that prayer had helped their loved ones survive.

At Orlando Regional Medical Center in Orlando, Florida, chaplains are part of the trauma team, and one doctor even admits to praying for his patients. When risky surgeries turn out well, he calls them miracles. This is certainly evidence that the medical community is beginning to recognize, or, at the very least, be open to, the concept that prayer works to bring about change or positive circumstances in the healing of patients.

Prayer is a demonstration of positive thinking being expressed to a higher intelligence. Our positive thoughts and desires carry strong vibrations that travel out into the ethers to effect change in others who share time with us in this existence. Sometimes those thoughts can be used to convey healing.

During the early 1980s, when June Schmitt was living in Los Angeles, California, she was involved in a group healing circle that worked with several doctors from UCLA and, on occasion, some well-known doctors from Texas. The doctors would bring their patients to the home where the healing group met. Many of the patients were affluent business people, although no names were ever revealed. For the procedure, patients were asked to lie on a massage table, and the healing group would psychically determine what they felt was medically wrong. After they located the affected area, they delivered healing prayers and directed healing energy to the patients.

The doctors then met with the healers and shared their feelings regarding the accuracy of the healers' diagnoses, and later provided them with the results of the healings. The accuracy rate was 100 percent for the diagnosis portion, and 75 percent for the improvements gained by the patients from the healings, depending upon the severity of the illness and its progression.

June Schmitt now resides in Cassadaga, Florida. She is a practicing medium, healer, and teacher of spiritual development and healing.

Healing prayer can be used to effect a change in the health of an individual at a distance. This is called *absentee healing*, and is accomplished by one or more people sending healing energies through their thoughts to people at a distance. It is not important to know the person with an illness to effect positive health changes, nor is it necessary to be a spiritual healer. The following story emphasizes that point.

Mattie J. T. Stepanek is a boy who suffers from a rare form of muscular dystrophy, which has already taken the lives of his three siblings. Being a great admirer of Oprah Winfrey, one of Mattie's requests when he was bedridden and thought to be near death was to share his message of peace and hope with Oprah through his book of poetry, *Journey Through Heartsongs.* His wish was granted, and as a result of his appearance on Oprah's television show, Mattie's book rose to the top of the *New York Times* fiction best-seller list.

When Mattie met Oprah, she was greatly impressed and moved by him. Consequently, Oprah later asked her audience to pray for Mattie after he developed a sore on the back of his head that was inoperable due to his precarious health. Oprah stated that she would report back in six weeks about Mattie's progress after receiving the audience's prayers. The result of millions of people praying for Mattie was that his sore healed, demonstrating to Oprah's viewers that prayer really works.

Healing prayers can take time to work a miracle for someone ailing, or there may be an immediate result from our prayers. A very dear friend of mine in Glendale, Wisconsin, named Carol Roberts, is a medium and teacher of psychic development in that area. Carol has experienced some very evidential results from prayer. Here are more examples of how effective our prayers can be, as experienced by Carol.

In the 1990s, Carol was conducting healing prayer circles for members of the public who were interested in participating. Approximately sixty-five people were sitting in one particular session. Carol began by directing the group in meditation, and then followed with healing prayers. Everyone who was seated in the circle prepared to project absentee healing to those in need. Individual members of the group who wanted to participate stated the name of the person to whom he or she wished to send healing, speaking the name into the healing circle.

A woman named Judith approached Carol with a special request. Judith wanted Carol to put her mother's name into the circle because her mother was not improving after a recent surgery. The mother was not eating, and Judith was afraid that if her mother didn't start eating, she would lose her. Carol agreed that they should all send prayers and healing energy immediately. So Carol verbally placed the name of the mother into the circle.

The meditation started at about 8:30 that evening. Carol created a beautiful healing energy by calling on the healing angels and God to heal those whose names had been placed into the circle. This took about a half hour to accomplish. Afterward, everyone stayed around to mingle and enjoy refreshments prior to going home. About twenty minutes after Carol returned to her home, the phone rang. It was Judith wanting to share an amazing experience with her.

Judith told Carol that when she walked in the door of her home after the prayer circle, she saw her little mother in the kitchen cooking! Judith asked her mother what she was doing. Her mother replied that she didn't know, but a half hour ago she became so hungry that she couldn't stay in bed and felt compelled to get up and make something to eat.

Carol continued with her healing classes, offering them for five-week periods one night a week in her office. One of her devoted attendees, Sue, called Carol prior to class one night, stating that she would not be able to attend because her doctor had discovered a suspicious lump in her breast, and the following morning they were going to remove the lump in the hospital. She was so upset she didn't think she could possibly attend the class. But Carol encouraged her to come anyway, expressing that when something this important is occurring, she really belonged in the class. Sue came to the circle.

After asking Sue for her permission to discuss her situation, Carol explained to the group that Sue had a suspicious lump in her breast, and asked the group to direct healing energy to her. The following morning Sue called Carol from the hospital. Sue told Carol, "You'll never believe this, but I was scheduled for surgery, and they did another exam and could not find the lump! The doctors did more exams and tests, and declared that the lump was gone." This is certainly evidence of the power of prayer! The disappearance of a breast lump occurred again in class for another woman after the group sent healing energy to her.

Sometimes our prayers may be beneficial in assisting loved ones when they are making their transition from life on earth to life in the spirit world. When Carol's mother was eighty-six years old, she began to fade physically. She had been ill with Parkinson's disease and arthritis for a long time. Carol arranged for a nice lady to stay with her mother during the day, since her mother insisted on living alone. At some point in her illness, Carol's mother shared her fears of dying with her daughter. She talked about a time when she was young that she had heard tales about people being buried alive. Carol quickly assured her mother that she would go peacefully in her sleep, and that she would pray for that to occur. Thereafter, when her mother asked how she would die, Carol always told her that they would pray about that, too, but assured her that she would just sleep peacefully away into the night.

One evening the lady caregiver telephoned Carol to tell her that her mother was not well and vomiting, so Carol drove to her mother's house. When she arrived, her mother told Carol to go home, assuring her that she was feeling much better, so Carol returned home. Around 3 a.m. the next morning, the caregiver called Carol to say that she had decided to spend the night, and had just checked on her mother in bed; when she had observed her in her sleep, she felt that Carol's mother had passed away. Carol and her husband rushed over to the house and found that, indeed, she had passed away. It was obvious that she had had a very peaceful transition, judging by the gentle expression on her face.

Carol phoned the church to ask for the last rights to be given. For years her mother had scrubbed floors and done everything conceivable for the church with a group of other dedicated women, so she felt the priest would hasten over. However, he said that he would "catch her in the morning" in the morgue. Carol was so hurt and angry by this remark that she told her husband that the two of them were going to give her mother the last rights.

Removing the last rights cross from the wall, Carol moved the opening to expose the holy oil and blessed candles contained within. She placed everything alongside the bed, took the oil, and anointed her mother; she then placed the little candles inside the cross in the designated places and lit the candles.

Carol and her husband stood at the foot of the bed, and Carol began to pray out loud for her mother's soul. She asked her mother to let her know that she was okay. At that very moment, one of the candles began to go crazy. The flame flickered from side to side, and then grew in height and brightness. There was a beautiful aura from the glow around the crucifix and the candles that were in the cross. Carol's husband grew nervous, backing away from the bed.

Carol said aloud, "Mom, I know you're here, I know you're safe." As soon as Carol spoke the last word, the candle immediately diminished in size and became calm again. Carol knew her prayers had been answered, that her mother had heard her. She continued the prayers and finished just before the funeral home attendants arrived.

Kristy Westbrook, an acquaintance of mine who is also from Wisconsin, is a psychic artist, a hypnotherapist, and a Reiki healer by profession. She once had the opportunity to assist a soul as it crossed over to the spirit world. The story began with the baptism of her nephew at the age of three months. Kristy and her husband were asked to be the godparents of this boy, but since they were already godparents to his older sibling, Kristy suggested that another aunt, Mary, be chosen. Mary was in the process of seeking to change her life, and was delighted to be given this honor.

Unfortunately, several weeks after the baptism, she committed suicide by shooting herself in the head.

Following Mary's death, the newly baptized infant became quite irritable. One night, in order to calm their irritable child, the parents placed him in bed with them. That night the father of the infant dreamed about Mary. In the dream she poked him and said, "Wake up! Your son is ready to fall off the bed."

The father awoke with a start and looked toward the end of the bed. He realized that the baby was, in fact, ready to fall off the edge of the bed, and quickly rescued the child by grabbing him and pulling him into his arms. From this experience they concluded that Mary was hanging around the baby and taking her godmother role very seriously.

Another peculiar incident happened when Kristy and the mother of the infant went to a psychic fair. While Kristy held the baby, the mother went to receive a psychic reading. Before the mother even sat down, the medium told her that a woman in spirit with an injury to her head was hovering around the baby. When the mother shared this information with her husband, he immediately saw this as validation that Mary was indeed hanging around the infant. Because Mary was so unsettled when on the earth plane, the father felt that her presence around the infant was also the reason the baby's disposition had changed.

Kristy was asked to lead a prayer circle for the purpose of alleviating the situation. Several people who knew Mary were asked to participate. The group in the healing circle quickly discovered that Mary was quite unwilling to leave. They felt that her leaving was complicated by the fact that she had two living children, both under the age of fifteen. Kristy tried to convince Mary to cross over to the light by telling her that she would be healed, and then when she chose to visit in the future, she would bring positive energy with her. After much cajoling and discussion, reluctantly, Mary left. Afterward, the baby recovered from his restlessness.

What about the prayers that we pray with earnest zeal for our own benefit that never appear to be answered? Does this mean that God turns a deaf ear to some prayer requests and listens intently to others? No. God treats all of us equally. There are no favorites, special people, or chosen ones. We are all special and chosen at some point in the many lives that we live. God would not choose to listen to one and ignore another. That simply would not be fair, nor would that be a demonstration of love. God is love, above all other things. The answer to any prayer will come at the perfect time and in the most appropriate way. The answer received, however, may not be the one we are anticipating.

Sometimes the answer to a prayer is "no." We may not literally hear the "no" delivered to us, but when our request does not manifest as we had prayed, it is a "no" we are receiving. For instance, how many times have we vigorously prayed to receive a promotion at work, only to find ourselves not so entitled? This does not necessarily mean God thinks we are unworthy of a promotion. It may mean that it is time to seek employment elsewhere, in a company that has better benefits and provides a higher rate of pay. One could interpret that to mean a resounding "yes!" to moving on with your life rather than staying stagnant in the old job. *Turn it around to the positive.*

On the other hand, if we were to contemplate the "no" answer, we just might discover that we really weren't deserving. Maybe there is a lesson to be learned in the present place of employment that we haven't discovered yet or are refusing to face. For example, perhaps you have been employed at the company for one year, and the one who received the promotion has been working there for six years. That could explain a lot. Are we honestly looking at our own qualifications or job performance? Perhaps the "no" answer is truly justified.

Try to see the wisdom of something not manifesting as we thought it should.

Lorie and her husband, Ben, had one small child and another on the way. They decided it was time to purchase a home for their growing family, rather than continuing to rent an apartment, and prayed for that event. The couple found a builder and put money down on a new home, then excitedly waited for it to be built. Lorie e-mailed pictures of the house's progress to those at a distance. Then came the terrorist attacks on September 11. At the time, Ben was a pilot working for a small airline. The airline industry suffered tremendously after the attacks, and there were many layoffs. Since Ben was newly hired, he was the first to be laid off. Lorie and Ben were devastated by this turn of events, realizing that they couldn't buy their new home. Fortunately, the couple received their investment back on the house, due to Ben's unemployment. All the while they prayed for help.

After a couple of months, good fortune struck the family, and their prayers were answered. Ben received a job offer in another state as a flight instructor, and the new job paid significantly better money. The family moved, and six months later they bought a lovely older home. In retrospect, Lorie could easily see that the new house wasn't meant to be. She also remembered that her brother, a former construction worker, had told her that he didn't think the workmanship was very good. The couple quite possibly could have been disappointed in their investment had they purchased the new home. After the terrorist attacks and the subsequent loss of Ben's job, Ben and Lorie thought their worlds had caved in. But everything worked out for the best for them.

Sometimes a "no" answer is the best answer for our situation. We may not understand that while we are praying for our desired outcome to manifest, so we must learn to trust in the process. The Universe has a bigger, better plan for us. Everything really will work out for our highest and best good. *Flow with events.*

Prayer Exercises

It is a wonderful practice to pray for others. In doing so, we help people accomplish their endeavors and gain spiritual support during crises. There are many opportunities for prayers that you may not have considered. You will find that many people will cross your path who need your prayers. Suppose you are cooking dinner one evening while watching the local news, and a story comes on about a house fire that totally devastated an elderly man's home. To add to his misery, the poor man has no insurance and is now homeless. This is an opportunity for you to send prayers to an individual who is in need.

Review the following exercises and try to incorporate the suggested activities of prayer into your daily life. Become aware of the vast opportunities for prayer when they are presented.

1. Pray for someone who has harmed you or treated you unfairly, and pray for those who cause you pain. Make this a regular part of your meditation.

2. Pray for adverse situations in the world to improve, such as wars or famine, and pray that people will learn to see things differently in order to bring about change.

3. Pray for those who require healing, strength, love, or whatever appears to be lacking. Ask God to send abundant love to all concerned so they may manifest their highest and best outcomes now.

4. You might want to pray for our world leaders, doctors, or whomever you feel so moved to send your prayers to, asking that they be wise in their decisions and act with love, not animosity. Ask that they be shown the way to open their hearts to help all of humankind.

5. Let prayer enter your life on a daily basis. Say prayers as you drive to work or while riding on the subway. Pray for the homeless woman on the street corner who is begging for a handout. Ask that she receive her highest and best now. Pray for the drunk man in the gutter to gain the strength to seek help. Pray for strangers who inspire your sympathy and have a void that needs to be filled. Ask that they attain their highest and best now.

6. Pray for little children you come upon who appear shabbily dressed or unkempt. Ask that the parents be able to express love to the children in spite of their hard times, and that the parents and children be delivered into a more prosperous condition now.

7. Pray for a family with three young toddlers coming out of a pawn shop who obviously just sold one of their valuables to ensure the family's survival. Ask that their highest and best be delivered now, in the form that is most suited to their particular condition.

8. Deliver prayers for our animal kingdom as well. Pray for the animals in your local shelter who are waiting to be adopted into homes. Pray for the feral cats in your neighborhood. Send prayers to the veterinarian who

established a mobile pet clinic that specializes in spaying and neutering cats and dogs. Ask that God bless all creatures, big and small, and keep them safe within a loving hand.

9. As an ambulance speeds by you as you are driving, say a prayer for the person who is being transported to the hospital. Do the same when you see fire trucks racing to someone's home. Ask for God's blessings upon the situation, and to bring the highest and best resolution now. Ask for blessings for the ambulance driver, the paramedics, and the firemen.

10. Say a prayer for the deceased when you see a funeral procession, and also for those who mourn the loss of their loved one. Pray for the soul of the deceased to realize truth and be healed. Pray for the loved ones to experience an easy grief, and that they receive understanding of the wisdom behind the passing of the one they mourn.

11. If you learn of a small business in financial trouble, send prayers for a speedy recovery, and pray that the owner be shown the wisdom to bring the recovery about.

12. If words do not come to you easily when creating prayers, simply pray silently to yourself, saying, "Bless your heart," or, "God bless you." The results will still manifest. Your good intentions are all that matter.

Chapter 11

The Balanced Observer

I once had a spiritual teacher who believed we should aspire to remain in a neutral position. She said we should not allow ourselves to become extremely excited due to a happy event occurring in our lives, nor go into a deep depression due to a sorrowful event. The idea was for our mood to be consistent. When I heard that I thought, How dull. I like being excited, gleeful over some wonderful event occurring. I don't care much for feelings of depression, but joy—now that's something I wouldn't want to sacrifice.

We can all remember feeling pure joy over circumstances such as receiving our first car, graduating from high school and college, getting the job we wanted, finding someone we thought was a perfect love match for us, and receiving special presents. Pure happiness rushed over us, our hearts swelled with joy, and a smile split our faces into rosy plums for cheeks. Who would want to give up those wonderful feelings and remain in neutral?

In the years since then, I have come to realize that she was attempting to teach us to be balanced in our approach to life, to be what I now call a Balanced Observer. It is being able to stand in neutral and see the truth in any situation. It is being able to see the bigger picture rather than being deluded by appearances. One could say it means rising above and looking down upon any given situation from a point of wisdom—the helicopter view. It would be appropriate to call this demeanor *centered*. It isn't easy to attain this centered position, especially if we happen to be passionate about something, or about life in general. In all probability, it is a lifelong project for most of us to achieve Balanced Observer status. After all, we are all works in progress, striving to be better. This balanced state doesn't come easily, and at times we can expect to falter in our efforts. But that's okay because we're human.

When we are able to participate as the Balanced Observer, it is very rewarding. It seems to make so much sense to us to be living the role of a Balanced Observer. We are aware that we are totally in charge of our reactions and thoughts, and this makes us feel so proud of ourselves. When confronted with something that would have upset us in the past, the words or situations now simply roll off our backs. The situation isn't important enough to react to. There is no effect upon our emotions.

During the times when our reach falls short due to our emotional natures and occasional attacks of temper, we have allowed our egos to get in the way. No matter how hard we try, that human quality rears its ugly head at times, obstructing our view of truth. We all share that boat on occasion: our egos try to block our view of the spiritual shore. But that's okay, because what we're experiencing is another opportunity to grow.

I believe that most people share my feelings of outrage when we, or someone we know, is treated differently, being shown undo favoritism. It smacks at our sense of fairness and what we believe is right action. At times like these, our Balanced Observer status is being challenged.

A couple of years ago an older friend of mine, Mona, was living in a beachside retirement community where she experienced unfairness. She decided to run for a board position in her homeowners association. In order to qualify for elections, Mona had to be active in her community. That certainly was not a problem for her, since she had been volunteering regularly at social events and other functions. Out of all the people who submitted their intent to run for the board, Mona was the only one who was denied the privilege to run for election. Her chances of winning a position were high since she was so well known and well liked. It was an obvious political ploy, devised by her competitors already on the board, to keep her out of the elections. Knowing this, Mona was hurt by the incident, furious, and, consequently, didn't even attend the election meeting. No Balanced Observer was present in Mona that day!

As the year went by, Mona saw the wisdom hidden in this unfair action. She came to believe she had been spared much grief. The elected board went through some stressful events that no one would have wanted to experience. Accusations flew all over the place, much infighting occurred, and the community developed bad feelings toward many of the board members.

The following year, when the time came to qualify to run for elections, a record number of people submitted their intent due to their dissatisfaction with the board. Mona was not one of those people. Some of the candidates were questionable, as their qualifications did not meet the criteria; one candidate had been conspicuously absent the whole year! However, everyone was approved to run.

Where was Mona's Balanced Observer during this issue? Standing proudly! This unfairly orchestrated election didn't bother Mona because she saw the situation for what it was. Mona was able to see the truth because her ego and sensitivity to fairness didn't block her vision this time. It also helped that Mona's life had taken a different direction, and because of this she no longer desired a position on the board.

If we can simply remember that everything works out for our highest and best interests, we can accept a disappointment more easily. In retrospect, Mona was happy not to be in a position that, even in good times, would have been stressful.

Many people care greatly about what other people think of them, placing tremendous importance upon being seen a certain way. When someone tells a falsehood about them, they become quite upset. How dare they say that! It's simply not true! Why, what will everyone think? Sometimes we just can't allow ourselves to care about what other people think. Our true friends will know a rumor isn't true, and our enemies will revel in the deceit. If we make an issue of the situation, we just fan the flame of the lie, much to the delight of our enemies. If we say nothing, everyone forgets about it quickly. Why project energy into a lie so it continues to grow? By not responding to the situation, it dies, much to the disappointment of our enemies. The lie dies. Nothing can live without energy. A Balanced Observer sees the truth in a situation and does not react. By keeping our egos out of the scenario, we become centered.

There is a scene in the movie *To Kill a Mockingbird* in which Mr. Ewell spits in the face of Atticus Finch, an attorney. A tense moment follows as we watch to see how the proper Atticus will respond to the other man's insult. Atticus stares at the defiant man, and the audience wonders what thoughts are scampering around in Atticus's brain. Then he wipes his face of the spittle, and proceeds to get in his car and drive away. He does nothing.

Atticus knows that it is useless to physically fight with Mr. Ewell, even though he towers over the man. Mr. Ewell is a poor, ignorant drunkard with a bad temper. No good could ever come from beating the man senseless for spitting in his face. Mr. Ewell will never understand why Atticus defended a black man or be able to realize that he needs to change his ways to improve his existence. Therefore, satisfying his ego by punching Mr. Ewell serves no valid purpose for Atticus. He sees the situation for exactly what it is and responds as a Balanced Observer.

Perception, as with all things in life, is also key here. How one person views an issue can differ greatly from how a second individual views the same issue if it affects him or her directly. We are more inclined to respond emotionally when it involves us personally. However, if a situation happens to another person, we can easily see it for what it is because we have an objective viewpoint.

When Sue laments about her lousy boss, her friend, Diane, can clearly see the truth in the situation because she has the benefit of impartiality. Diane knows that Sue has a tendency to be tardy in most situations. She also knows that Sue is horribly disorganized, which gives her a clue that perhaps the boss isn't actually lousy; rather, he simply wants Sue to arrive on time and be more organized. Diane can also intuit from Sue's conversations that her boss may need to acquire some better communication skills when dealing with Sue. Diane is standing in the neutral corner, a Balanced Observer. Her perception is not hindered by obstructions.

When we are faced with challenging situations, we need to stop ourselves from reacting before we do something we have a good chance of regretting. This is where those affirmation reminders can be very helpful. When we catch ourselves reacting, we need to stop ourselves quickly and run the most appropriate affirmation reminder through our thoughts. Perhaps "Release rigidity to God" is an appropriate affirmation. Run that reminder through your head a couple of times, and step back from the situation for a minute. Then ask yourself, How can I see this differently?

Sometimes pulling ourselves up short is really hard to do because we are attached to the outcome and, frankly, we don't want to detach and be neutral. We are so wrapped up in our egos and the outcome of a situation that we can actually feel ourselves resisting the detachment. However, these are the times we most need to pay attention and detach from our surroundings. Once we detach, we can be the Balanced Observer in the situation. We respond from a point of neutrality and not one of reaction. Therefore, we respond properly, from that centered place within. When we do this, we feel so proud of ourselves, and we see the truth in the situation. We also receive a bonus because we discover that the situation was actually pretty minor, and wasn't worth getting so upset about.

It is wise to ask ourselves one little question when we are confronted with a situation that requires us to either react with our ego or respond as a Balanced Observer: will this be important in five years? In all likelihood, the answer will be "no." It probably won't even be important in five hours. Therefore, it isn't worth it to become upset, angry, or to say something stupid that we will regret later.

Often when we attempt to force things to bend our way we find later that we are not happy with the outcome. Yes, at the time it appears that this is what we want. But is this a desire that is in our best interests, or is our ego talking?

Sometimes we do everything within our human power to force the issue, perhaps manipulating people and situations to our advantage. We allow our egos to rule supreme, pushing our personal agenda in the face of others. We are rising to the challenge and we want to win. As a result of fighting for what we want under these circumstances, we frequently decide afterward that the prize wasn't what we really wanted and wasn't worth the fight. The reason this happens is because what we desired wasn't in our best interests, and we were ignoring our intuitions when they were nagging at us to halt. If you find that you have to fight an intense battle to get what you want, you need to step back and ask yourself, Do I really want this? What price must I pay to win? The idea is to trust in the process and surrender attachment to the outcome when faced with this kind of challenging situation. *Flow with events.*

When we are attempting to accomplish something and it isn't going well, we also need to consider that this might be a sign telling us not to proceed. We are given signs in life for the purpose of guiding us, but we have to pay attention in order to recognize when the sign is being thrust at us. Everything happens for a reason. The Universe sends us messages that we are to follow for our best interests. When we ignore them, unpleasant issues occur and we aren't happy. In retrospect, we think, Why didn't I pay attention? All the signs were there.

Many people believe that if something isn't proceeding smoothly, we need to back away and go in a different direction. They see this as a sign that it is not meant to be. This is the law of nonresistance. If we place ourselves in the Balanced Observer stance, we can read the signs the Universe is sending us when we need to change directions. If we have not placed an expectation on the results, it is far easier to do this.

Joyce was divorced and alone. She wanted very much to be married to a decent man, but had only stumbled across less than acceptable mates. One night after her meditation, she told God that she wanted to be married and prayed for this to happen. The way she phrased the request made all the difference.

> Dear God, I want to be married. But if this is not the best plan for me at this time in my life, I understand and accept that. If I am meant to be married again, please send the right man to me now. If I am not to be married at this time, then I will wholly accept whatever outcome is best for me. I put my trust and faith in Your hands.

What Joyce demonstrated is how to surrender the results of a prayer to the Universe. She relinquished her attachment to the outcome of her sincerely delivered prayer. She believed that whatever happened would be for her highest and best interest. As a result of her earnest prayer, one month later she met her future husband the very first day she started a new job. *Trust in the process.*

A lovely woman named Freda came to me for a spiritual reading recently. She exemplified what it means to flow with events. Her view of life was to take it as it is presented, and not fight for outcomes or attempt to force things to go her way. If she is met with an obstacle, she interprets the block to mean that she is to go in another direction. Consequently, Freda is leading a very happy life. She doesn't get upset over small things. Most things in life aren't important enough to her to allow herself to become angry or disturbed.

The law of nonresistance suggests that we allow ourselves to be open to flowing with the tide. It is a feminine attribute to be open and receptive. When we allow ourselves to be receptive, we attract positive energy from the Universe. We are saying to the Universe, "Here I am, an open receptacle; use me as a channel for good."

By placing ourselves in a neutral position, we are allowing ourselves to be balanced, understanding that things may or may not work out the way we think they should. Either way the situation sways is fine, and is as it should be. Five years from now, we will have forgotten the whole issue. We are placing our trust in the process of our lives, that the Universe has a divine plan that will benefit us when the time is right. We only have to be open and receptive to receive. Again, we are reminded of the cup of water. An empty, open cup receives from the Universe. *Flow with events.* It makes life so much easier!

While on our paths to becoming Balanced Observers, we should have noticed so-called coincidences occurring, along with a synchronicity of events. To begin with, *there is no such thing as a coincidence.* Banish the word "coincidence" from your vocabulary. Everything happens for a reason! *Everything!* The Universe runs in a finely tuned order that assists us in all our endeavors.

My husband, Vincent, bought a small house as an investment property in a little town near the city in which we live. Once he made improvements, he planned to sell the house. One night while we were dining at a local Chinese restaurant, Agnes, a woman from my yoga class, walked in. She came over to our table, and I introduced her to my husband. Because she lives in the town where the house is located, my husband asked Agnes some questions about the neighborhood. In the course of their conversation, Agnes told Vincent that the cook who works in her restaurant lives next to his house and is interested in purchasing it, if he wants to sell.

That is an excellent example of what most people would call a coincidence. But Agnes lives ten miles north of the Chinese restaurant. For her to have chosen to eat at the restaurant we were in when there are three other Chinese takeout restaurants within two blocks of each other on her way home was not happenstance. She chose the one we were in because the Universe had a plan. Later on, Vincent did sell the house to the cook.

My husband has been involved in a lot of seemingly coincidental situations. Awhile ago he was researching the possibility of purchasing a tax deed on a condominium located thirty miles from us. Just after discussing the condo with me, Vincent drove to a nationally known home improvement chain where he ran into a woman he hadn't seen in several years. While catching up on events, the woman told Vincent that she is on the board of trustees of the same condo complex in question. Consequently, Vincent was able to receive information about the condo board's attempts to foreclose on the unit. Coincidence? Hardly.

Everything happens for a reason. We are guided if we just learn to allow ourselves to be open to receive. The Universe is only too happy to assist in our lives so that we may better our existences. When our expectations are dashed and we learn later that it was for the best, we understand that there was a reason for a situation not working out the way we thought it should. The Universe was watching out for us. There was a good reason our hopes were dashed. The same is true with so-called coincidences. There are reasons why we unexpectedly run into people in restaurants or home improvement stores. The Universe is trying to help us put our lives in order.

Some people have a knack for drawing to themselves what they need. Arthur is that kind of person. It's as if the Universe overhears his thoughts and sends the solution. Just when Arthur needed a rare part for his antique boat, he saw the part advertised in the newspaper. Arthur needed information about a particular college, and within one week he was introduced to someone who had attended the same college. Arthur calls this knack to attract what he needs "putting the energy out there." Whenever Arthur has a need, the Universe supplies what is necessary to fulfill that need.

Synchronicity is when two things happen simultaneously. Again, some people would say this is merely a coincidence. However, I would encourage you to become aware of synchronistic events in your life and to recognize them for being the blessings they are, rather than mere coincidences. When we dismiss events as being coincidences, we are denying ourselves another opportunity for spiritual growth.

My favorite synchronistic happening is taken from my book *How to Communicate with Spirits.* One morning I asked my spirit teachers to give me direction about whether to pursue a particular writing project. That same afternoon I was driving to Daytona Beach on Interstate 4 with the radio blasting away. As I was about to make my exit, former Beatle George Harrison began singing "I Got My Mind Set On You." During the chorus he kept repeating "do it, do it, do it, do it." At the exact time he was singing the "do it" portion, a motorcyclist passed me on the left side. Printed in large black letters on the back of his tee shirt were the words "Do It." So, I did it!

Pay attention to synchronistic events. There is no such thing as a coincidence. When we believe in coincidence, we are placing a limit on the capacity of God to manifest what we need. God, Goddess, the Universe, is unlimited. As creations of God, we are also unlimited. Our thoughts assist in the process of creating events in our lives, in attracting to us that which we need to help us grow to be spiritual beings. We are special, and we are blessed. God loves us and is there, right *there,* to help us every step of the way. All we have to do is reach *in* to receive.

As you go about your day, you will notice people who are not happy. On some days they seem to be everywhere. Recently I was shopping for groceries after leaving yoga class. To my delight, I discovered a basket of cosmetics that were on clearance. While rummaging through the lipsticks, another woman joined me in the quest to find a bargain. I cheerily remarked to her that the lipsticks were L'Oréal, suggesting that we were receiving a real treat. Not only did she not look at me, she didn't even speak. It was as if I had been addressing the grocery basket. The woman continued to forage around, then selected a lipstick and left.

While I was going through the checkout lane, I projected a friendly attitude to the clerk, which is my normal behavior. I figure the clerks need to encounter as many positive people as possible to balance out the not-so-positive ones who roll through. By the end of the transaction, I had at least elicited a faint smile from her.

On the way home, I thought about all of the people who go through their days unhappy, bored, and miserable. And that's a shame. When we encounter people who appear to be unhappy, we should at least attempt to brighten their day. A smile, a kind word, or a sympathetic gesture can make all the difference in the world to a person who is feeling miserable or out of sync with his or her environment.

Anyone on the path to becoming a Balanced Observer would notice such a person and extend a ray of sunshine to brighten that person's day. Even if the person does not respond positively, his or her soul will have felt the positive intent. This is the business of a Balanced Observer: projecting positive energy to others whenever possible.

Exercise

1. Select a situation, problem, or difficult relationship in your life, and write one sentence in your journal describing it. For example: why does my husband have to watch sports on TV when we have a day off together instead of going out with me?

2. In your journal, answer the following question: how can I see this differently? Using your imagination and everything you know about the situation, problem, or person, list another perspective on this issue. For example: (a) he loves sports; (b) this is the only time he can watch sports programs; (c) my husband finds it relaxing to watch sports programs after a stressful week at work; or (d) he has a right to enjoy an activity that doesn't involve me.

3. List ways in which you can reach a compromise on this issue. For example: (a) I can go shopping, jogging, to the gym, or surf the Internet while he watches TV; (b) we can go out to dinner later; (c) we can do something together on another day during the weekend; or (d) I

can join him in the living room and read while he watches the game.

4. Create a reminder sign to instill the insight you have gained by looking at this issue through different eyes. For example: my husband works hard and deserves to be happy.

To-Do Always

1. Begin your day: prior to getting out of bed, mentally review any of the affirmations you can remember from the signs you previously created. Let your affirmations wash over your sleepy body so they adhere to your subconscious mind. Prayer is also a very nice activity to do before rising; it's a positive way to begin your day.

2. First thing in the morning, perhaps during meditation or in the shower, ask yourself, How can I be of help to someone today? Be still and wait for an impression, a feeling, or an image that brings an answer to your question. During the day ask God to show you how to assist whomever may need your attention, be it a friend, relative, stranger, or coworker. Keep an open mind as you go through the course of your day, being aware of people who may be in need of your particular brand of love. See where you are led to be helpful. Perhaps your deed of spiritual service will be to use your umbrella to cover an elderly woman who is carrying a bag of groceries in the rain, walking her to her car. It may simply

be that you compliment a woman on her dress, thus brightening her day. We never know how we will affect people by delivering a small compliment. If their day had been particularly stressful, your flattering remark may be the spark that ignites them to throw off a bad mood. The bonus you receive from all these actions is a feeling of joy.

3. Continue journaling your thoughts, feelings, and dreams. When situations arise that are difficult, journal your way to the other side, where happiness is found.

4. Continue to be grateful for all events in your life. Keep a daily listing if you so choose.

5. What we give we receive. What do you want to receive now? Give that which you desire to someone or something, just as you would want it to be given to you. For example: suppose you want to receive a promotion at work. Reach out to someone who is lower down on the ladder of success than you and give him or her a hand up. This may be someone within your office or elsewhere who needs a boost. Assist that person in bettering his or her skills, presenting a better professional image, or giving him or her an opportunity to be noticed by a person in authority. Continue this giving as often as opportunities present themselves.

6. Be a peacemaker. When opportunities arise, be a mediator to two or more people who are having difficulty communicating with each other. Help them to reach a new

understanding. Be open to opportunities to assist people, without intruding, of course. Reconcile situations that have grown from nothing into something stupid, which would never have happened if the parties involved had kept their egos in check.

Afterword

Now you have all the instruments necessary to orchestrate your spiritual life into a beautiful symphony. Yes, it takes effort, but that sweet kind of effort you give when you are knowingly doing something positive. The end result has a bonus: you feel rewarded. A smile of satisfaction crosses your face and your heart feels happy. You know the feeling; you've already experienced it if you've been practicing the exercises!

Each day you will recognize new lessons when they are presented to you, provided you remain aware. In your possession are tools that can change so-called negative situations and circumstances into positive happenings. You have learned that you have the ability to choose to see things differently.

You are a work in progress, ever growing, like the rest of us. Your future life experiences will continue to provide you with valuable knowledge daily, weekly, yearly, and for the rest of your life. Pay attention! Life is not a series of coincidences, dumb luck, or random happenings. Our lives have purpose, even if we work in a position that is considered menial. Remember the power of one. One person can bring positive change to any circumstance, and that one person could be you, if you make the effort.

In summary, be about the business of spreading positive energy to all whom you come in contact with. Since we have choice, choose to be positive. If you have been practicing the exercises in this book, you already know how wonderful it feels to spread positive energy. And that's the beauty of it, the icing on the cake! You receive also.

Share your love. Why have we been gifted with the energy of love if it isn't meant to be shared? Jackie DeShannon wrote a song that was called "Put a Little Love in Your Heart." If we carry love in our hearts, it will spill out to other people. It simply cannot be contained! Besides, it's so much easier to love than to hate. Hate takes a lot of energy, and it makes us ill. Our bodies were not intended to hold hate, dislike, contempt, and other negative emotions. God meant us to be loving beings while experiencing this walk on the earth. Again, when we give love, we receive. More icing!

And while you're sharing that love, why not share your prosperity? When we give we receive so much more in return. However you choose to share, be it at church, a homeless shelter, or an animal sanctuary, it will make you feel wonderful. I follow the recommendation of the author

Catherine Ponder, who wrote *The Dynamic Laws of Prosperity*. I tithe 10 percent to my church. Every time I place money in the offertory, I feel so wonderful! I see this act as showing gratitude for what God has provided me. And the more that is provided, the greater the amount I tithe. You do not have to follow my specific example, but please share your prosperity somewhere. It returns again and again.

Release rigidity. Life on earth is way too short to be living it rigidly, so release it. It isn't making anyone happy, least of all, you. Remember that it won't be important next week, so why hold on to it? Just let it go. Focus on the positive. There's probably a lesson to be learned from whatever it is that is making you react in a rigid manner. Besides, you'll feel so much lighter and brighter. And, as an added bonus, your body will respond with improved health.

Be kind. Speak kindly. An old exercise is to replace the annoying person standing before us with a spiritual person. In our mind we visualize Buddha, Jesus, Brigit, Mary, or some other special being. Now, how would we speak to this person? With great respect, kindness, and love, of course.

Most of all, cause no pain. Please. There is too much pain in this world as it is, why add to it? What can we possible anticipate will be improved by causing another soul pain? They must learn their own lessons; it is not our purpose to sit in judgment of what another should or should not be doing. Focus on the positive. Dedicate yourself to being a beacon of positive energy. Let other people see your positive light beaming forth through all situations. When they see you holding the position of Balanced Observer, they will not respond adversely. You will have created a positive energy flow, and everyone will respond in kind.

If we continue to turn our gaze in the direction of positive, share our love and prosperity, act in a kindly manner, speak with kind words, and relax our bodies and minds, consequently, we will live a happier existence. I promise!

Namaste.

Appendix

Suggested Reading List

The books listed in this appendix are intended to be a sampling of what I personally feel are good spiritual books. Some of the books I have selected are considered to be spiritual classics, while others are newer to the market. It's a starting place that will, no doubt, lead you to discover other authors and other books. Some of the authors here have written more books than the ones listed. If an author strikes a spiritual cord within, by all means peruse a library or bookstore for other books by that author.

Spiritual Reading Material

Bodine, Echo. *A Still Small Voice.* Novato, Calif.: New World Library, 2001.

———. *Echoes of the Soul.* Novato, Calif.: New World Library, 1999.

Breathnach, Sarah Ban. *Simple Abundance*. New York: Warner Books, 1995.

Buckland, Raymond. *Doors to Other Worlds*. St. Paul, Minn.: Llewellyn Publications, 1993.

Dass, Ram. *Journey of Awakening: A Meditator's Guidebook*. New York: Bantam, 1990.

Dyer, Wayne W. *Manifest Your Destiny*. New York: Harper Collins, 1997.

———. *There's a Spiritual Solution to Every Problem*. New York: Harper Collins, 1997.

———. *Your Sacred Self*. New York: Harper Collins, 1996.

Edward, John. *Crossing Over*. San Diego, Calif.: Jodere Group, 2001.

Gawain, Shakti. *Creative Visualization*. Novato, Calif.: New World Library, 1978.

———. *Living in the Light*. Novato, Calif.: New World Library, 1998.

Owens, Elizabeth. *How to Communicate with Spirits*. St. Paul, Minn.: Llewellyn Publications, 2001.

Ponder, Catherine. *The Dynamic Laws of Prosperity*. Marina del Rey, Calif.: DeVorss Publications, 1985.

———. *The Millionaires of Genesis*. Marina del Rey, Calif.: DeVorss Publications, 1976.

Shinn, Frances Scovel. *The Game of Life and How to Play It*. Marina del Rey, Calif.: DeVorss Publications, 1941.

Walsch, Neale Donald. *Conversations with God*. New York: Putnam, 1996.

White, Stewart Edward. *The Betty Book*. New York: E. P. Dutton, 1937.

Williamson, Marianne. *A Return to Love*. New York: Harper/Perennial, 1992.

———. *Illuminata*. New York: Random House, 1994.

Inspirational Books

Moen, Larry. *Meditations for Awakening*. Naples, Fla.: U.S. Publishing, 1994.

———. *Meditations for Transformation*. Naples, Fla.: U.S. Publishing, 1994.

Rodegast, Pat, and Judith Stanton. *Emmanuel's Book: A Manual for Living Comfortably in the Cosmos*. New York: Bantam Books, 1987.

———. *Emmanuel's Book II: The Choice for Love*. New York: Bantam Books, 1987.

Stepanek, Mattie J. T. *Heartsongs*. New York: Hyperion Books, 2002.

———. *Journey through Heartsongs*. New York: Hyperion Books, 2002.

———. *Hope through Heartsongs*. New York: Hyperion Books, 2002.

———. *Loving through Heartsongs*. New York: Hyperion Books, 2002.

———. *Celebrate through Heartsongs*. New York: Hyperion Books, 2002.

Taylor, Herbe. *The Little Book of Miracles*. Rockport, Mass.: Element, 1995.

Index

☽ ORDER LLEWELLYN BOOKS TODAY!

*Llewellyn publishes hundreds of books on your favorite
subjects! To get these exciting books, including the ones on the following
pages, check your local bookstore or order them directly from Llewellyn.*

Order Online:
Visit our website at www.llewellyn.com, select your books, and
order them on our secure server.

Order by Phone:
- Call toll-free within the U.S. at 1-877-NEW-WRLD (1-877-639-9753). Call toll-free within Canada at 1-866-NEW-WRLD (1-866-639-9753)
- We accept VISA, MasterCard, and American Express

Order by Mail:
Send the full price of your order (MN residents add 7% sales tax) in
U.S. funds, plus postage & handling to:
> **Llewellyn Worldwide**
> **P.O. Box 64383, Dept. 0-7387-0423-7**
> **St. Paul, MN 55164-0383, U.S.A.**

Postage & Handling:
> **Standard** (U.S., Mexico, & Canada). If your order is:
>> Up to $25.00, add $3.50
>> $25.01 - $48.99, add $4.00
>> $49.00 and over, FREE STANDARD SHIPPING
> (Continental U.S. orders ship UPS. AK, HI, PR, & P.O.
> Boxes ship USPS 1st class. Mex. & Can. ship PMB.)
>
> **International Orders:**
>> **Surface Mail:** For orders of $20.00 or less, add $5
>> plus $1 per item ordered. For orders of $20.01 and
>> over, add $6 plus $1 per item ordered.
>>
>> **Air Mail:**
>> *Books:* Postage & Handling is equal to the total retail
>> price of all books in the order.
>> *Non-book items:* Add $5 for each item.

*Orders are processed within 2 business days. Please allow for normal
shipping time. Postage and handling rates subject to change.*

Women Celebrating Life
A Guide to Growth and Transformation

ELIZABETH OWENS

Change happens. Choose to celebrate the times of transition in your life with beautiful, empowering rituals, pampering baths, candles, scents, and music.

Have you ever noticed that certain birthdays are milestones and other birthdays are just markers of years gone by? Why not celebrate each birthday richly and fully? It is interesting that many rituals and traditions mark the passage from singlehood to married life, yet nothing but a divorce decree marks the transition from married life back to singlehood. Why not hold a Severing Ties Ritual?

Women Celebrating Life is your guide to celebrating change. You will find a ritual for every stage a woman may pass through on her life's journey:

- Welcome each birthday as your special day
- Greet the changes in your body
- Face difficult times of transition

Don't try to avoid the unavoidable. Come, celebrate the changes in your life!

1-56718-508-8, 140 pp., 7½ x 9⅛ $12.95

To order, call 1-877-NEW-WRLD
Prices subject to change without notice

How to Communicate with Spirits

ELIZABETH OWENS

Do you feel the friendly, subtle guidance of spirit beings and want to learn how to contact them directly? As a child, did you experience premonitions or ghostly visitations, and now desire to reestablish that spiritual connection? This practical text, written by a certified practicing medium, relates fantastic stories from real-life psychics that run the gamut of spiritual entity encounters. The author's friendly, authoritative voice will guide you through the basics of identifying and classifying spirit guides and other entities, and then show you ways to hone your skill at communicating with them. Nowhere else will you find a more complete and compelling set of anecdotes from noted professional mediums, each showing you how to effectively interact with your personal guides. This book will show you how to contact inhabitants residing in the mysterious world beyond our own.

1-56718-530-4, 216 pp., 5³⁄₁₆ x 8   **$9.95**